WOMAN UP

THE 21ST CENTURY WOMAN'S GUIDE TO FEELING
LIBERATED TO OWN YOUR SPACE, SPEAK UP FOR
YOURSELF, DECIDE WHAT YOU DEEPLY DESIRE,
SHAMELESSLY DECLARE IT TO THE WORLD AND
GO OUT AND GET IT!

JODIE SALT

AND CO.

CONTENTS

DEDICATION

To all the inspirational women in my life who have shaped me to be the woman that I am today, for good or bad, I thank you.

To my mum, Hilary - having you tell me how proud you are of me keeps my fire burning. I love that I am a carbon copy of you.

To my daughters - Leila, Amber and Sadie - this one's for you! You are my world. May my legacy be to create a world that is equal, full of opportunity and possibility. My one wish is for you to live freely as strong, independent women, who choose your own destiny and believe that anything you wish is possible. The world is your oyster! YOLO! #fuckthegaslighters

To Grandad Tom - you we're EPIC in encouraging the real me to shine!

To my biz bestie, Roxy - You've inspired a huge part of this journey, thank you for being my safe space and my reality check.

To my one and only BFF, Chloe - You started this and I owe this journey to you. The door is always open. I'd love you to return and finish it with me.

And finally, to my rock - My amazing hubby, David. Thank you for making me a braver person, for believing in me always, for loving me however I show up. You make me feel invincible when you're right beside me.

ABOUT THE AUTHOR

They broke the mould when they made Jodes. That's what her Grandad Tom always said.

Jodie Salt is an Executive Coach, Leadership Development Consultant, and expert in behavioural change. She specialises in coaching women to be more assertive.

She's not your textbook coach. A self-confessed, down-to-earth, northern lass. Don't be fooled by her casual approach, with over 15 years' experience in large, blue-chip organisations, she's more than worth her salt!

Frank, Infectious and Fun is how she's described by many and at the same time delivers amazing results for her clients, landing them promotions, catapulting their credibility, inflating their influence, and skyrocketing their results!

She's a fun-loving, belly-laughing, thrill-seeking mum of three daughters and wife to the amazing 'Saint David' (he must be to put up with all the female hormones!) as well as a troop of all female pets: Tilly-Mint the Goldendoodle, Dolly the Persian cat, Megan and Molly the bunnies and last but not least, Tony the Tortoise (don't ask!)

Her guilty pleasures in life are chasing rainbows, anything Parma Violet or salted caramel flavour, quaffing copious amounts of prosecco, general anaesthetics, and a lifelong obsession with Madonna (and a secret bit of Bieber).

Jodes has made it her mission in life to turn the notion of 'pretty' on its head - helping women to be known for the value and contribution they make, not just what they look like - Pretty Confident; Pretty Smart; Pretty Strong; Pretty Funny - whatever your version of pretty is.

ONE

INTRODUCTION

LET ME HAVE A LITTLE GUESS... Your life looks flippin' amazing on paper, right? You've got all the things going on. Decent house, pretty nice car, good job/business, reasonable amount of disposable income, settled in a relationship, maybe a small family, couple of holidays a year, meals out... But... and it's a BIG BUT.... You're just. not. feeling it.

You're fed up, tired of it all, 'done in', sick of the hamster wheel of life. Head down, stoically powering on through. You're not feeling happy, fulfilled or successful. Far from it! You feel like you've been dragged through a hedge backwards most days and flop onto the sofa at 9.30pm with a bottle of wine, thinking FML! And the worst of it all? Now you feel guilty for being unhappy. There are so many people far worse off than you! You ungrateful bitch! Get a fucking grip!

Sounds harsh, doesn't it? But you know it... That's how you talk to yourself. You'd never say that to a friend, but you'll happily berate yourself. And so, it continues. You swallow it.

Push it down deep. Stick your head in the sand while as each day passes you become a smidge more bitter, a tiny bit more twisted, a little more resentful. But you put on your 'game face' (literally) every morning and 'just get on with it'. Maybe you get treated like a doormat by those who are supposed to love you most. Maybe you're a people pleaser, putting your-self at the bottom of the list because that's easier than upset-ting the applecart or dealing with the drama. Maybe you're a moaning, nagging cow that everyone's fed up with. Maybe you're an eye roller, sulker, silent treatment giver, huffer puffer extraordinaire, mutterer of flippant and sarcastic comments under your breath. Maybe, just maybe, you're a bit of a bulldog chewing a wasp, barking and biting at people for the things that piss you off.

I want you to pause at this point. Look ahead to the future you. Do you want to become THAT woman? Like the mother-in-law from hell? The one who drives you insane? Who makes your blood boil? Who interferes in EVERYTHING? Yeah, well, that's where you're heading. That's you in 25 years if you carry on as you are. If you continue to PUT UP & SHUT UP.... Or you could CHOOSE to WOMAN UP!

What? How dare I? I say this with love because you only get one shot at this game. As my dad once kindly told me...

 "Life is not a dress rehearsal you know."

The reason that I dare? Because that was me too - I've been there, done that and got the flippin' t-shirt! And the good news? There really is some - actually, screw 'good' - amazeballs news.... I got out of this! Even better... I can get you out of this!

It's time to Woman Up. Now, before you go getting your knickers in a twist, it's not what you think it is... quit jumping to conclusions and making assumptions already (I'll talk to you about that later, btw), we're only a page in, gimme a chance woman!

I'm asking you to come with me on a journey. I'm asking you to put the graft in. Do the shizzle. Learn the lessons. Make it happen. And that? That doesn't come EASY. What's wrong with society? We've lost the ability to do HARD STUFF. We want everything to be easy and we want it all dropped off by the Amazon delivery driver NOW.

TOUGH TITTY.

This doesn't work like that. So, unless you're ready to roll your sleeves up, get down and dirty with me (believe me, it's gonna get messy - there'll be snot and tears (and few belly laughs)) and get stuck in, you might as well put this book back on the shelf, or gift it to someone who you'll be jealous of this time next year (that is a promise).

I will let you in on one secret... the killer ingredient that this whole book is underpinned by... What every 21st century woman should possess but cannot be bought. We are not born with it, yet we have the capacity to possess it in abundance. It is a skill that ANYONE can learn:

It's called Assertiveness.

Need to know a bit more before you commit to going ALL IN with me? Fair dos. What makes me the expert anyway? How will you know I'm "The One"? I'll tell you.

1. I'm a woman and a pretty decent one at that (I'm smart, clever and funny AF. Oh, and I bake mean scones and a lemon meringue pie to die for!)
2. I've been through some crap in my life (I'll dish the dirt throughout this book don't worry, you'll get all the juicy goss.)
3. I'm a qualified Executive Coach, specialist in leadership development & behavioural change – I've been helping women smash glass ceilings, navigate the boys club mentality and grow their credibility in corporate careers for over 15 years.
4. I've been on my own development journey to becoming assertive and it cost me in excess of £20K in courses, coaching, research & development, and I don't want it to have to cost you the same.
5. I'm passionate AF about women speaking up for themselves, knowing what they want and going out and getting it without any guilt! I'm sick of women allowing themselves to be doormats, people pleasers, keeping quiet to keep the peace, scared of upsetting anyone or worrying what other people think. I'm pissed off that they get labelled as "too emotional" when they stand for something important to them. It grates on me that the gender pay gap still isn't addressed and we don't have equality in the boardroom. I'm utterly fuming that we don't feel safe walking home at night, that we're still objectified, that people think they can talk about our bodies and the way we should or shouldn't look and that we're sexually harassed and cat called around every street corner. ENOUGH! I want women to be skilled at

standing up for themselves, finding their own voice,
be able to say No to things they don't want to do and
smash any glass ceiling they set their heart on! Oh,
and #instagramlife is pure bullshit! #getoffthegram

If you're wondering how this book will benefit you, let me
make it really clear and simple for you.... do the work and
implement the actions and you will feel LIBERATED! Would
that be good? I've not had any woman tell me to this day that
they don't long to experience that feeling. It's the feeling that
makes you feel weightless and free, all the hairs stand up on
your neck and your arms. A sense of letting go, possibility,
opportunity and joy. A vibe of excitement, mischievousness
and adventure. It's like being on Ecstasy without the worry of
"Have I taken a bad pill?" (Apparently, so I've heard).

I'm living proof that this stuff works. I've worked with many
women, not just female execs - entrepreneurs, stay at home
mums, women doing the 9-5, ladies what lunch, empty
nesters... And I've plans to take it to the next generation of
women, our teenagers and daughters.

My big promise to you is for you to finally feel liberated to
own your space, speak up for yourself, decide what you
deeply desire, shamelessly declare it to the world and go out
and get it!

How will we do this? Here's the main stop off points on our
journey together...

The Backdrop:

- What got us here won't get us there - the cultural and historical backdrop.
- What it really means to Woman Up and to be assertive (I guarantee, it's not what you think).
- The common mistakes women make.
- The mindsets for success.
- The Art of Womanifesting... and a very important lesson from Hannah Montana!

Identity:

- Rediscover the true you and reconnect with the girl you were born to be.
- Rewriting the stories and limiting beliefs that have tainted you over the years and held you back.
- Building confidence, self-esteem and self-worth to feel like somebody, instead of nobody.
- Learning to get out of your own way and stop the self-sabotage and finally step into the authentic and best version of you.

Power:

- Understanding and taking back your power so you can own your own space.
- Figuring out what you really want, what you deeply desire and unashamedly declaring that to the world, without guilt.

- Developing your personal boundaries, learning to say NO.
- And finally letting go of giving a shit what other people think of you.

Communication:

- How to use what your mama gave you to get yourself heard (tip: it 's not your tits).
- Land your messages with impact and have influence over others, whether that be in your personal or work life.
- Overcoming waffleitits (yes, it's an actual 'thing') and being succinct, getting to the point quickly and powerfully.

Emotion:

- Turning emotion to your advantage so you're not labelled as 'too emotional'.
- Navigating hormones without losing your shit (including the dreaded M word - that's menopause for those of you who don't need to think about it yet).
- Handling conflict, confrontation and challenge easily and beautifully.
- Exploring shame, vulnerability, anger, resentment and the green-eyed monster.
- Developing resilience, tenacity and grit.

Relationships:

- The relationship with yourself - self respect & self compassion.
- Meeting your needs and understanding the needs of others.
- Dealing with toxic relationships and gaslighting, and how to end them.
- We'll even talk about becoming more assertive in the bedroom!

Credibility:

- Get taken seriously by family, friends, colleagues and stakeholders.
- Get things done faster, cheaper, and with greater engagement by fostering high trust.
- Give great, high-quality feedback that inspires people to do better.
- Become skilful at operating in your zone of genius and surrounding yourself with the right people.

Luminary:

- Having gravitas, commanding an audience, turning heads when you walk into a room (without being all tits and teeth about it).
- Championing and cheerleading other women, networking collaboratively not competitively.
- Inspiring the next generation of women.

I have a clear objective for you in this book, a set of criteria to measure whether it's done its job or not. That criteria is made up of five key things. It must achieve at least one, but ideally all five.

1. To educate you;
2. To empower you;
3. To entertain you;
4. To inspire you;
5. To liberate you.

Finger crossed. I'll check in with you at the end on these.

So, my invitation to you is to step on into my space with me. Go ahead. Turn the page and start your own transformation.... It's time for you to Woman Up!

———

What if the Hokey Cokey really is what it's all about?

Before we start... an important message:

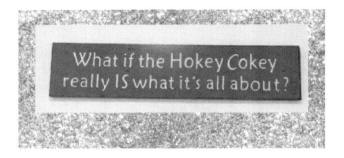

In my downstairs loo at home, we have this sign up on the wall. I bought it when on a hen do in York about 5 years ago, simply because it made me laugh... and think.... Where did that saying come from and what does it mean? What IF the Hokey Cokey REALLY is what it's all about? I've been meaning to write about it for sometime and that day has finally come.

I loved this song (and dance) as a child and enthusiastically took part in it at many a birthday party (my kids think I've lost it if I sing it now, they have absolutely no idea!) But it was just a bit of fun, right?

As the natural curious child we all once were, I remember asking someone what it was about and what did it mean? I was met with "It's just a silly song". Now I'm older and I'm even more freakin curious! So, I thought I'd take some time out (I was supposed to be being mindful and as usual my mind wandered off and I failed to rein it back in!) to dissemi-nate my version of what it means. So here goes...

The process is all about putting body parts 'in' and 'out' starting off quite timidly with the odd arm and building up to the whole body which suggests to me a sense of testing out and gradual immersion in something... life perhaps?

After each body part has been in and out a few times, we shake it all about, do the Hokey Cokey and turn around – an interesting part of the process. This could translate into the evaluation of a particular life experience. The putting in and out of the body part is the experience. The shake it all about maybe illustrating the exit and 'shake off' of the experience. The Hokey Cokey being the reflection on the experience and the turn around being the conclusions we draw and the recalibration as we come back to face the circle, refreshed with our newfound learning to inform the next experience along the journey.

And for me, that is what it's all about. Life is about experiences. We grow as we expose ourselves to more experiences (put more body parts in) and take the time to step back, reflect, draw lessons and conclusions and then use those to inform us and serve us well for future experiences. This applies whether those experiences are good or bad. The good ones are easy. You like it so you want to do it more. The bad ones are where it gets interesting. I've always lived true to the saying:

 "What doesn't kill you makes you stronger."

A few more people could benefit from this premise. A lot of people simply run away and hide from those and don't actually DO the Hokey Cokey with them, and therefore, they don't grow. It's tough and uncomfortable, but to lead that happy, fulfilling, and successful life, it's important that we reflect after the experience, draw lessons and conclusions, and use them for next time.

So, back to the question... What if the Hokey Cokey really is what it's all about?

Well, if my interpretation is anything to go by, then the Hokey Cokey REALLY is what it's all about! If you really want to lead a happy, fulfilling, and successful life then YOLO! Chuck yourself head first into as many experiences as you can. The scarier the better! AND then make sure, whether you had a blast or shit yourself, you take the time to step out, reflect, learn, recalibrate and then throw yourself back in!

It's easier said than done! I experience it myself – I put off doing something because I'm scared of what might happen. Luckily for me, I've got Roxy (my biz bestie) behind me who just pushes me in, and that's what I need sometimes.

I'd like you to do the Hokey Cokey with this book. That way, you'll get the best out of it. Now go and add it to your playlist!

TWO

WHAT BROUGHT US HERE WON'T GET US THERE: THE BACKDROP

The Future is Female

THINGS HAVE CHANGED over the years. Women are standing up for their rights and what they deserve so much more, but there's still a way to go. Yes, protests, demonstrations, marches and petitions are all good at making some noise, but the only way culture and society really change is when individual people decide to DO something different. We're all familiar with the saying:

 "Actions speak louder than words."

Feminism has evolved. No longer is it all about women burning their bras! It's a strong global movement that involves EVERYBODY, not just women. But it's important that we play our part and become masters of our own destiny. Being "done to" is a thing of the past! And while we're at it, let's just be super clear about what feminism means. There's a lot of hate out there for the word. Many folk will show an aversion to feminism but, in the same breath, say they believe in equality. Feminism is fundamentality about equality between the sexes. Now let's not get confused... equality is not sameness. It is not being treated the same - because we're different, and that's a good thing. Equality is about equal rights and equal opportunities. Just because a man might be physically stronger than a woman (or vice versa), doesn't mean they are any less equal when it comes to rights or opportunities, but they are different.

AND there's still a huge gender pay gap to be bridged. If we want to be valued for the contribution we make and the talent we possess more than for what we look like, then it's time to let actions speak louder than words. It's time to invest in our capability and personal development like we do in our appearance. Let's show the world we mean business by proving where we spend our energy, effort, time and money!

First, let me say I'm not against men - I like them... a lot! But what do I mean by 'the future is female'? One of my biggest idols right now is Jacinda Arden, the 40th Prime Minister of New Zealand, but probably not for the obvious reasons. Yes, she's successful, and she balanced having a baby with being Prime Minister! But I admire her because she is skilled. She's highly skilled at decision making, influencing, having presence and personal impact, building trust, leading change... the list goes on. Women have an abundance of latent potential - potential that we're just not tapping into. We've got so much value to add with skills that come much more naturally, in my view, to women than to men. I'm talking about things like being more collaborative than competitive, being brilliant relationship builders and networkers and being highly emotionally intelligent.

The world is changing. People are changing. Businesses are changing. That means the way we do things needs to change too. Take a basic work example. The traditional autocratic leadership style is no longer serving of most organisations. Why? Because, even before the turn of the century, we were no longer paid to "do", we were paid to "think". In 1959, Peter Drucker, coined the term "Knowledge Worker" in his book, "Landmarks of Tomorrow". He suggested "the most valuable asset of a 21st-century institution, whether business or non-business, will be its knowledge workers and their productivity." From a Wikipedia article on the subject, "Knowledge workers are workers whose main capital is knowledge. Examples include software engineers, physicians, pharmacists, architects, engineers, scientists, public accountants, lawyers, and academics, whose job is to "think for a living". Barking out orders just didn't cut the mustard any more. We started to see the emergence of a more democratic and coaching style of leadership in the early part of the noughties. But hey, don't park your arse and get too comfy there, because we've whizzed through that era too! Nobody needs to have knowledge anymore. That's what Google is for, right? Don't even get me started on what we teach in schools in the UK these days - it's beyond me! Why we're still teaching knowledge and testing memory recall is flippin crackers if you ask me! Especially when we've got a generation of teenagers who struggle to make beans on toast and figure out how to get a bus or a train somewhere. We're now in an era of "Learning Workers" not "Knowledge Workers". That means we're paid for figuring shit out, solving problems, being innovative and creative, crafting relationships and collaborations - all the stuff that comes naturally to us gals! Now is our time! We need leaders of businesses, institutions, organisations and families to lead with the heart, with emotion, connection, collaboration, inspiration and empowerment... and that needs a healthy dose of female contribution to make that happen.

Let's no longer be "done to", told what we should be, how to behave, where we belong. Let's step up to the plate, declare our commitment and make our contribution. There's no room for victim behaviour, only highly accountable behaviour - we make things happen for ourselves. So, what got us here, won't get us there. It's time for a new approach - you ready?

———

A little bit about me

I'm not going to drop everything here and spill my life story, Jeez Louise, you'll be using this book as toilet roll before the end of this section! Ha! Nah, I'm actually not that boring as it goes. Tbh, I'm quite good fun and I do have some pretty funny stories to tell. But I'll sprinkle them throughout the book so it doesn't look like it's all about me, hey? Note to self... the purpose of this book is to help the reader, not indulge the author (Who am I kidding!).

On a serious note, it probably is worth me shedding a bit of light (and shade) onto how I came to be an expert on assertiveness and the path my life has taken. I will keep it brief here though.

My main career has been a corporate one, always in the Learning and Development field. I've been training people how to do various jobs, skills and more recently, behaviours, all my working life, from being a "stand in" call centre induction trainer when I was 18 (courtesy of my very first and fabulous boss - big shoutout to Jo Benson). The latter years have been spent working in Leadership Development as that's where I stumbled upon my passion and trained as an Executive Coach.

However, rewind slightly to a time when I was leading Learning and Development teams. I got into managing at quite a young age. I was only 20 when I was first appointed into a Training Manager role. Looking back, whoever gave me that job (I do know but I won't name and shame him) was a complete dick! I was awful! I thought I was the bee's knees at the time but came to learn much later in life when I bumped into an old colleague at a christening (obvs. she'd had a few sherbets) that EVERYONE in the office knew I'd only been given the job because I was the "nice bit of totty". Everyone except me, that was. I took some time out to have my first two daughters. When I went back to work afterwards (different place) at 26, I had a very traumatic experience.

Long story short and without going into detail, I was on the receiving end of what I can only describe as quite aggressive, erring on bullying, behaviour by one of my direct reports. Really smart kinda bullying. Not the obvious stuff. It was constant interaction with aggression (or often passive aggressive) and I had no idea how to handle it. It got to the point where ironically, they raised a grievance against me for bullying them! I toyed with the notion of jacking it in and walking away but I've always been one of those people... you know the ones I mean... that if you tell them they can't do something, they do it twice and take pictures... yeah, that's me! Something in me wouldn't be beaten by it. So, I took myself off to London on an assertiveness course to learn how to deal with the situation. It cost £2000 for a one-day course (plus travelling expenses) but it taught me one simple technique that liberated me. (I'll show you the technique in a little video which you can access from the FREE resources download link - bit.ly/woman-up-FREE-resources). I went back to work, tried it and it only went and flippin worked, didn't it! GET IN!!!! I was on a roll. So, I invested in a personal coach to help me with my continued development. I spent a small fortune! So, I fell in love with assertiveness at that point.

A subsequent role had me operating at a much more senior level, training and coaching more senior leaders and having stakeholders that were at 'the big cheese' status. Some of these guys were absolute arseholes, complete twats even. There was this one guy, head of site, who found it completely acceptable to holler all kinds of inappropriate crap across a call centre floor at me – in fact, he took great joy in it. The call centre floor had approximately 500 people on it, and he would make his comments whilst I was escorting visitors around the place #rude. In the monthly management meetings in the board-room, we'd place bets before the meeting started about who was gonna be in the firing line that week. Anyway, I found these situations really challenging to handle and one of my colleagues, who later became my bff, used to support me. Big shoutout to Lady Rimberts, aka Chlomo. She was as hard as nails. She didn't really care what anyone else thought. She took nothing personally and gave as good as she got. Over time, she really helped me to grow a thicker skin, to not take things as personally, to let go of the bullshit, to say what it was that I wanted to say. She helped me to grow and own my space, to be confident in my own skin and stand up for myself. I'll be thankful to her for that forever.

I soon came to realise that I was sick and tired of coaching people who didn't really want to be coached. I also really didn't enjoy coaching grey suited men who thought they were already brilliant and had nothing to learn. Yet, I discovered that the women I was coaching at a senior level lit me up! It was more than just 'strategy' or 'leading change'. It was about them as a woman: Their confidence. How they felt. Their friendships. How they looked. Their health and wellbeing.

That's how Ladies Life Lounge was born with my biz bestie, Roxy, and I continue to help women develop their assertiveness to smash glass ceilings, grow their credibility and influence, know what they truly desire and go out and get it, through The Woman Up Way, my signature programme!

Things is... it's earned me a bit of a reputation... I now get likened to someone... Who do you think that might be? You'll never guess it, not in a million years! On the face of it you might think it's not a very appealing association, but there's a bit of depth to it that I really like.

I've been told I'm like Nanny McPhee!

WTF? I know! Here's the good bit though. When I explored why I was likened to Nanny McPhee I got this response.... "Well, Nanny McPhee has a saying, doesn't she, that she tells all the kids and the same can be said for you Jodes...."

 "When you need me but do not want me, then I must stay. When you want me, but no longer need me, then I must go."

What's that all about then? Well, I take this as a huge compliment tbh. It's quite uncomfortable in the early stages of working with me. Not because I'm an arsehole or anything, but because we do the deep work on you and that can be a bit squirmy and feel like you're sat in a bath of beans (my worst nightmare, I'll tell you about my phobia of baked beans another day). My job is to encourage you to sit in that bath of beans, to have a good feel around in it, maybe lick bean juice off your fingers (now I'm retching at the thought...), maybe even swim backstroke through the beans! However, by the time we're done, you've enjoyed my company, become a new woman, had THE BEST TIME EVER and you LOVE me SOOOOOO much you don't want me to leave!

THREE
WHAT DOES IT MEAN TO 'WOMAN UP'?

What Does Woman Up Mean?

LET'S kick off by giving you absolute clarity on what Woman Up ACTUALLY means.

Not what you think! The natural assumption is to link it to the phrase 'Man Up'; a phrase that has probably crippled thousands of men's' mental health over the years. That's not it. I'm certainly not about to cast the same pressure and shame onto women.

Woman Up means to rise and to elevate women. To bring women onto a level playing field. To have the same rights and opportunities as anyone else, not just men. It means to step into your own space, own your life, be a master of your own destiny, reconnect with your true identity, find your voice, know what you want and go out and get it.

I said this before, no amount of protests or petitions or talking on chat shows about this stuff will create the kind of change we need to see in our quest for equality. Culture only changes when individual people decide to DO something different.

Ok, so if you haven't figured it out already, then this book is all about one killer skill that every 21st century women should possess - the art of assertiveness. It's one of those words that is commonly misconstrued. People tend to have a very wonky definition of what it really means. So, before we begin and delve into the detail, let's get crystal clear and have super clarity on what we mean by assertive.

Sometimes, it's useful to begin with what it is not. So, let's bust some of those myths right now. The classic misconception is what it looks like. When you ask people to bring to mind an image of an assertive woman, most people describe someone in a boldly coloured trouser suit (otherwise known as the power suit, with 80's shoulder pads and usually red), arms folded, scowly/steely look on her face, red lipstick and sky-high stilettos. What a crock of shit! Just look at these pics of me. Would you say this is an assertive woman?

Yes. And not a stiletto in sight! (For the life of me, I can't bloody walk in them.) You'll mostly see me in pastel colours, floaty numbers, jumpsuits, trainers and slogan tees!

This is closely followed by what it sounds like. For the record, it is NOT any of the following:

- Being bossy;
- Telling it how it is;
- Calling a spade, a spade;
- Being forceful;
- Demanding behaviour.

Instead, let's define the true meaning of assertiveness and start as we mean to go on. In fact, the definition alone might change EVERYTHING for you! Here goes:

- To be able to stand up for your own or other's rights in a calm and positive way;
- Someone who behaves confidently and is not frightened to say what they want;
- Positive and confident in a persistent way;
- Someone who states their needs, wants and opinions clearly so that others take notice;
- It is a skill that can be learned.

Let's explore a couple of these points in a little more detail...

Many people come to me wanting to be assertive but hold the belief that "it's just not them"; they weren't born that way. Well, let's quash that one right now. Because it is a skill. And that means it doesn't matter whether you were born with it or not (although some of the most assertive people I know are under the age of 5). You can learn it. That immediately makes it accessible to everyone. The absolute beauty about it too is that you can style it your own, authentic way.

There are some key words and phrases in some of those definition bullets above that I want to explicitly land with you.

Notice how it's not just about you. It's about being able to stand up for your own and other's rights. That means not walking past stuff that's not acceptable. Just because it isn't happening to you, doesn't make it none of your business. When it comes to things like racism, sexism, harassment, bullying, victimisation (to name but a few), it's super important that we speak up, and that's part of being assertive. Interestingly though, it's followed by the words "in a calm and positive way'. We all know that saying:

 "It's not what you say, it's how you say it."

This is not license to start ranting, raving and kicking off left, right and centre. Let's just be clear on 'positive' while we're at it. Positive isn't about being all jazz hands and happy-clappy like a circus seal. Positive, in this context, means that it is solution focused, accountable and kind.

Now, the second and third points use the word 'confident'. Many of us go through life constantly being advised by others to "just be a bit more confident". Let's just clear this little matter up right now: THAT'S NOT HELPFUL ADVICE! I'm sure we'd all love to "just be a bit more confident"! Sadly, we weren't all born with a magic switch on our backs, nor can we pop it in our basket whilst we're picking up a few 'bits' from Waitrose on the way home from work!! Confidence is a state. It's not a skill in it's own right. To be ABLE to demonstrate confidence, we need to feel skilled (able & capable) to do the task in hand. Therefore, in order to not feel frightened and instead feel confident, it requires us to have developed the 'skill' of being assertive.

There's one trait that I see in mega decline as time goes by, and that's persistence - you know, a good old dose of tenacity, a GIRL WITH GRIT! I LOVE Angela Duckworth's book, "Grit". We live in a society now that is driven by EASE. We want everything to be easy. Jeez, just look at how we shop for Pete's sake! (Who is Pete anyway?) You can have a little button at the side of your loo now that if you press it, the Amazon guy fetches some more loo roll round in a jiffy! If anything is remotely taxing, difficult or hard, we throw the towel in. Being assertive involves not giving up at the first hurdle. Let's take a simple example of a conversation with someone where you're trying to get them to come round to your way of thinking. I have had many a coaching conversation with my clients in this scenario and it goes a little something like this...

Me: What did you say or do to influence the situation?

Them: I told them {blah, blah, blah}.

Me: Ok, and then what?

Them: Well, they didn't do it/said no.

Me: And then what did you do?

Them: I said it again and they still didn't do it.

Me: And what did you do after that?

Them: What do you mean? Nothing. I left it.

Me: Did you have another go? Try something different?

Them: No, it was too hard, I gave up, didn't see the point.

You know by now that I love a good saying. Well, here's another one.... I think it was Einstein that said;

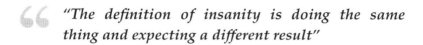

"The definition of insanity is doing the same thing and expecting a different result"

I'm also a fan of another one that kids prove to us brilliantly:

"Persistence beats resistance."

I don't think I need to say any more, do I? You get the picture. If we want to create change and get what we want, we gotta dig deep, go again, try harder, mix it up a bit, try a different approach but above all, don't give up!

My three teenage daughters are a classic sign of the times. On many occasions, they'll come to me with something they want to do and I'll say "Great, off you go then," and they'll respond with something like this

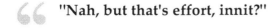

"Nah, but that's effort, innit?"

Even when that's about making a cheese sandwich or going upstairs to get some socks! We've lost the art of effort. We might as well all give up now if we can't be arsed! NO! I won't allow that to happen! It's my mission in life to create a movement of effort - of perseverance, tenacity and an army of GIRLS WITH GRIT!

Finally, on this topic of definition, I'd like to draw on the phrase "states their needs, wants and opinions clearly so that others take notice". Two things - needs and wants. They are two very different things, and you are allowed to have both. I'd recommend knowing what's what for you though; what you class as a need and what you class as a want. Opinions are also up there as being mightily valid.

Latterly, and this is the important bit, that you can state these clearly so that others take notice. Here's where, as women, we often trip ourselves up. On the bit about being clear, the female of the species often suffers from a condition I like to call 'waffleitis' - the inability to be succinct. We go around the houses and use 27,000 words when 6 would do! When it comes to getting people to take notice, I go back to Einstein....... Instead of risking being slapped with the 'nagging' label, it's time to have some influence. This is actually a secondary skill to being assertive (I'll be offering up some tools and techniques to help you with this later in the book). At a basic level, this is about tailoring your message to the recipient, speaking their language, working in their currency, using specific strategies to influence them round to your way of thinking. NB - this is different to persuading, negotiating or manipulating... we can do better than that!

I'd like to conclude this section by pulling all of that together into a simplistic form. When you boil it down, there's just two ingredients to assertiveness - consideration and courage. Notice how consideration comes first. The consideration to listen to the other person's wants and needs, followed by the courage to state your own.

I depict this in a model, based on an original created by Ernst in 1971, called OK Corral. It's a concept that is at the core of Transactional Analysis and is the concept of OK-ness.

OK-ness has been variously used to describe a philosophy of how we regard other people (Berne, 1972/1975), a frame of reference governing a person's whole outlook on life (op. cit.), and the minute-by-minute behavioural responses to what happens to us (Ernst, 1971).

It shows the four basic positions we can occupy in terms of the way we view ourselves and others. We can be either OK or Not OK with ourselves, and either OK or Not OK with the other person.

It also aligns beautifully to the work of Stephen Covey in his book, The 7 Habits of Highly Effective People, specifically Habit 4: Think Win-Win.

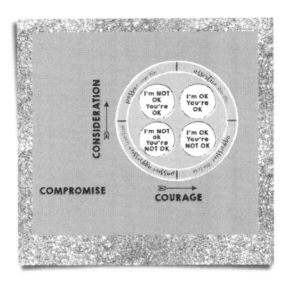

Here's what I want to you notice and take in from this:

- Assertiveness is win-win thinking. We both work hard to satisfy each others wants and needs as well as our own and believe that both is possible. It starts with 'listen first' i.e., consideration before courage. It requires us to have the capacity and ability to collaborate rather than compete. One does not have to be at the expense of the other. (I cover more on collaboration in Chapter 5 on Power).
- Aggressiveness is either when courage comes before consideration or we don't care about the other person at all - we ditch consideration entirely. We go straight in with our mouths open and our ears closed. We're on our own agenda and single-mindedly focused on getting what we want. Now, sometimes it might sound

forceful, loud, brash, pushy, bull in a china shop -
those are the overt sign of aggressiveness. But it can
also come in disguise. It can appear quite palatable on
the surface, so don't be fooled into thinking that just
because it's said with a smile, it doesn't constitute
aggressiveness.

- Many women identify with being passive - they have
  an abundance of consideration and very little courage.
  They're the doormats and people pleasers of life.
  Always putting others' needs before their own.
  Always the one that goes without and settles for less.
  Makes for a Cinderella style life - one that is lacking
  happiness, fulfilment and success.

- Now then... Passive aggressive. Often overlooked and
  very few people identify with this BUT SOOOO many
  people display it! It's the lose-lose zone. Nobody gets
  what they want or need. I know! You're sitting there
  thinking "Well, which numpties are daft enough to
  hang out there?" Most of us! Especially women! Here's
  what it typically looks like: (Give yourself a point for
  every one of these you do)

- Eye rolling;
- Huffing and puffing around the place;
- Saying "I'm fine" when you're clearly not;
- Sulking;
- Giving people the silent treatment;
- Moaning about someone to someone else;
- Being two faced;
- Winding people up;

How many did you get? (Although don't be chuffed with yourself if you got loads of points, this one works more like the TV show Pointless.)

- The biggy... COMPROMISE. We've all been brought up being told to compromise. I'm about to break the news to you that compromise is SHIT! Now, hang on.... Hear me out! There's method in my madness. When we compromise, we both give up something in terms of what we stated were our wants and needs, therefore, nobody truly 'wins'. In fact, we both lose. Now, I know I've wound you up there. Sorry, couldn't resist (that's me being passive aggressive), so let me be clear. I'm not saying we should never compromise. It's helpful sometimes. But what I am saying is that if we're assertive enough, there is a better, higher alternative. When we both have high degrees of consideration and courage the magic happens! We're able to achieve outcomes that we didn't believe were possible before. That can be in many different ways. Sometimes we achieve the absolute epitome and work together and find a way for both of us to get what we need / want - bingo! In others, we open our minds to new ways of thinking, new perspectives, we're influenced, have our minds changed, realise that what we thought we wanted and needed wasn't what we want and need after all! It's something completely different and is totally achievable! BOOM! I know you're probably still a bit sceptical. That's ok. Stick with me throughout the book and I'll show you the art of the possible so that you can create the evidence for yourself that it works.

OK, so there you have it. In a nutshell (albeit a big one), what it means to be assertive. As a reminder, this is the skill that underpins what it means to Woman Up and the methodology in The Woman Up Way which we'll be delving into over the coming sections within this chapter.

———

The Assertive Bill of Rights

I want to share with you early on in this journey, something that was a complete revelation to me and changed my life in a nanosecond. That something was The Assertive Bill of Rights.

So, just let me roll back a little bit. In the early days of my assertiveness journey, I understood what it took to be assertive, I had a decent grasp of the concept. You know, I got it. However, something was massively holding me back from living it out. I didn't BELIEVE that it was OK for me to be like this; that I had permission, license, THE RIGHT. Until this came into my life. This was a major moment of LIBERATION and, as I mentioned in the introduction to this book, that is one of my success criteria for you - to feel liberated. So, it's important I share this with you early on, to give you the acceleration and boost out of the starting blocks to set you up for success and keep you engaged with me, hungry to learn more!

So, let's just recap.... Being assertive involves expressing your thoughts, feelings, wants and needs, while respecting and listening to the person you are talking to. It also means recognising that other people have the right to express the same. Communicating assertively can help us feel understood, increase confidence, and decrease conflict. The following rights highlight the freedom you have to stand up for yourself and be clear about your position, without disrespecting others.

Enter the Bill of Assertive Rights, developed by Manuel J. Smith Ph.D., author of "When I Say No, I Feel Guilty: How to Cope - Using the Skills of Systematic Assertive Therapy". This list of rights reminds each of us that we have the right to determine what is best for us on our own terms. When we consistently behave in an assertive manner to advocate for our own freedom to choose, we reinforce our value.

Many of the ideas now associated with assertiveness training were first proposed in Smith's book, published in 1975. The book explains that assertiveness is largely about expressing oneself clearly and resisting manipulation. It proclaims a ten-point 'Bill of Assertive Rights', all based around one key principle:

> *"The right to be the final judge of yourself is the prime assertive right which allows self-determination."*

(This bill of rights has evolved in different hands over time and you may come across slightly different or more elaborate versions of it, in terms of language used.)

1. I have the right to have and express opinions, views and ideas which may or may not be different from other peoples - and so do you.
2. I have the right to have these opinions, views and ideas listened to and respected (not necessarily agreed with or 'put on a pedestal', but accepted as being valid) - and so do you.
3. I have the right to have needs and wants that may be different from other peoples - and so do you.
4. I have the right to ask (not demand) that others respond to my needs and wants - and so do you.
5. I have the right to refuse a request without feeling

guilty or selfish - and so do you.

6. I have the right to have feelings and to express them assertively if I so choose - and so do you.

7. I have the right to be 'human' (to be wrong sometimes) - and so do you.

8. I have the right to decide not to assert myself (to choose not to raise a particular issue) - and so do you.

9. I have the right to be true to my own self; this may be the same as, or different from, what others would like me to be (including choosing friends, interests etc.) - and so do you.

10. I have the right to have others respect my rights - and so do you.

You can download this as a print to frame and put on your wall to remind yourself every day from the Woman Up Way FREE resources section here: bit.ly/woman-up-FREE-resources

Before you move on and turn the page, I encourage you to do a quick exercise for me (actually, not for me at all, for YOU) ... Go and stand in front of a mirror (or if you're feeling brave, record a little selfie video), look yourself in the eye and read aloud those ten statements to yourself with conviction. In the next section, we're going to be talking about mindset, and believing in these rights is a huge and important step to setting yourself up for success in having the right mindset in place.

PS. If you do a video, I'd LOVE to see it! You can happily share it with me in private in my DMs on Instagram or, if you're feeling super brave, post it to your stories, tag me in it and slap the hashtag #womanupinprogress on it! I might even send you a prize!

———

The 3 Woman Up Mindsets

I always start with mindset in everything I teach and coach. Why? Because it's like the foundation of a house - it holds everything up. In fact, I'm gonna go for my fave analogy when it comes to mindset and that's an iceberg. As humans we are remarkably similar to icebergs. Really? Yes really!

You see, only a third of an iceberg is visible above the surface - you know this, of course. And that 2/3 of it is hidden below water away from view. Well, we're the same. Let me explain before you think I've gone nuts.

We meet each other at a behavioural level - you only get to see my behaviour and I only get to see yours. We use what we see behaviourally to judge each other, however, we judge ourselves by our intent. Immediate mismatch. Our intent sits below the surface with a whole bunch of other stuff like our values, thoughts, feelings, experiences and beliefs - beliefs about ourselves, other people, the society we live in, the world! All of this stuff makes up our 'mindset' and is like our anchor, grounding us. But above, up on the surface, it is attached to a buoy. That buoy is our behaviour. Our behaviour is driven by, or anchored to, our mindset. That's why when you try to make changes within yourself superficially, at behavioural level, like going to the gym, it doesn't stick. To make sustainable, 'sticky', lasting change, we must first alter ourselves at mindset level, fundamentally, the things we believe.

Wonky or crappy mindsets mean we get in our own way of being fabulously happy, fulfilled and successful.

For a significant number of women (not all, but many, me included), there's a lot we could do to get out of our own way. There are some specific mindsets that would help us to create the space to live the happy, fulfilling and successful life we all deserve, and the shift in action we would take as a result would make such a big difference to those women who may not be in the fortunate position that we are too – for example, those in domestic violence situations. Those mindsets are:

- **Presence** – Being more present is about connection, an energy, being in the moment and noticing without being noticeable. Sounds bizarre I know! It's more than just paying attention and not being on your phone. People with presence have gravitas, influence, command an audience, turn heads when they walk into a room. We need more women like that who can drive change; who demonstrate the authority and credibility to compel others to follow. More on this in Chapter 9: Credibility.
- **Accountability** – In a world full of blame, excuses and sticking our heads in the sand there's never been a more desperate time for high accountability. True accountability is more than just calling people out if they've not done something or kept a promise; it's an attitude. Unaccountable people live life in victim mode – 'things happen to them'. They are the mood hoovers and Deidre Downers of life. They have no influence and people avoid them. Sometimes, they have a really valid point, but nobody will listen because they're perceived as negative. Accountable people, on the other hand, are the folk who make shit happen –

'things happen because of them'. They're the people who acknowledge the reality of the situation, they take ownership for it and themselves, they find solutions and most importantly, they execute. They take purposeful action and get the job done.

- **Courage** – as an assertiveness coach, I spend most of my time coaching passive women. We now know that assertiveness has just two ingredients – consideration and courage. These women have bucket loads of consideration but lack the courage to state their own wants and needs. Instead, they become doormats and people pleasers. Being brave and courageous is about firstly knowing what you want (a stumbling block for many), and then believing you have the right to ask for it and deserve to get it. The women that do attempt it often overplay it, because they only have a male as a role model upon which to base the behaviour on, which translates into the alpha female bitch from hell as she tips the balance to aggressiveness. We all know one. Most despise her. And that's sad, because she stuck her head above the parapet, she went for it, she was brave, she committed to her dreams and aspirations and now she's likely feeling quite isolated and lonely. A small minority have mastered the balance and got it nailed and when you meet her, you know about it. She inspires you from the moment she walks into the room. And no, she's not necessarily dressed in a power suit with stilettos and bright red lipstick! Remember those myths we busted?

So, my mission is to help more women like you get out of your own way by developing these three mindsets, first and foremost. Once we've nailed that, then we can focus on the skills and behaviours to help you be successful in your own, authentic way, whether that be smashing the glass ceiling, getting a seat at the board table, breaking through the boys club mentality, getting a promotion, quitting the 9-5 and becoming an entrepreneur, having a happy relationship with your partner, being a guilt free mum, ditching toxic friendships or even having a wonderful relationship with your mother-in-law – can you imagine? By the end of this book, you'll be nailing it!

———

The Art of Womanifesting - the 7-step model to Woman Up

Womanifest: (adj.)

When a woman uses her innate force of powerful feminine energy to make shit happen.

In March 2020, my business with Roxy, Ladies Life lounge, hosted the most epic women's lifestyle and empowerment show that the North of England has ever seen, at the iconic Hilton Deansgate hotel in Manchester, where we brought over 1000 women together for a weekend of education, entertainment, empowerment, inspiration and liberation. Now, they're five tall orders by anyone's standards and we smashed it! The feedback was off the charts! It was called Womanifest - a festival of all things female, feminine and womanly. We loved the definition of this word (see above). It describes everything we're both about. Most importantly, it specifically articulates what my personal work is all about. It's my mission, day in day out, to not only help other women to use their innate force of feminine energy to make shit happen, but also to do it for myself!

But it's a bit of a weird word, right? It doesn't yet exist in the English dictionary but I'm determined to make that happen! So, if I tell you to go sort your life out by womanifesting some shit, would you know what to do? I thought not. I'm kinda glad about that though, because it means I get to define it. I've been spending the last few years of my life working on creating some methodology behind this and the job of this book is to enlighten you into that.

Womanifesting is the process we go through on our Woman Up journey (must credit this to the fabulous wordsmith that is Joh Foster - I was on a LIVE one day and couldn't articulate the verb for Woman Up and she helped me out on this one - cheers Joh!)

The first thing I want to be clear about is that it's got nothing to do with manifesting, at least, not in the sense that most people assume. It's become a bit of a buzz word, particularly in the entrepreneurial space of late, but I find it really irritating. Why? Because it's hugely misrepresented and misunderstood. There's a couple of different definitions for manifesting. The most common one being the spiritual definition:

"Spiritual Manifestation is the theory that through regular meditation and positive, constructive thought, you can make your dreams and desires become reality. Spiritual manifestation revolves around the New Age concept of the Law of Attraction. Simplified down to a single statement, the Law of Attraction states that if you think and act in a positive way, good things will happen to you, but if you think and act negatively, bad things will happen to you." I'm good with it at this level.

Spiritual manifestation holds that if you really want something and truly believe it's possible, it will happen. On the other hand, if you dwell on what you don't want to happen, giving it lots of thought and attention, that will probably happen, too.

This is where it starts to get a bit sticky for me.

Manifestation operates on three levels: the spiritual, the psychological, and the physical.

On the spiritual level, it is believed that thoughts have an energy of their own, which attracts whatever the person is thinking of. This energy itself is neither positive nor negative - it simply is. In order to harness this energy to your benefit, one must practice four things:

1. Know what you want.
2. Ask the universe for it.
3. Feel and behave as if the object of your desire is on its way.
4. Be open to receiving it.

I'm all on board with point 1 (more on that later). After that, you've lost me. Ask the feckin' universe??? Nah. All a bit too 'woohoo' for my liking. Things only happen when you actually DO something. You have to take ACTION.

Now, what I can get on board with is the psychological level where it is considered a form of the "self-fulfilling prophecy". If I am convinced my dreams and desires are unattainable, I will only make a half-hearted attempt, be overly receptive to any obstacles as a sign of impending failure, and eventually become discouraged and give up - True dat.

On the other hand, if I am convinced my dreams and desires are attainable, even inevitable, I will react differently. I will throw myself into the task, working hard to achieve my dream. I will view obstacles only as temporary setbacks - a stumbling block rather than a road block - and view any sign of success as proof that my dreams are slowly becoming reality - a more scientific and tangible explanation being 'confirmation bias'.

Finally, on a physical level, I'm back to the "are you sure about that" position on this one. At a basic level it suggests that the bio-chemical processes in the brain e.g., the firing of neurons being transmitted between different synapses (thousands of them, btw) are creating a tiny magnetic field, and the magnetic waves within that field carry content that allow us to control our thoughts. This theory has not yet been proven. (I've totally 'top lined' that as I'm not neuroscientist although I'd like to be one day and it is on my vision board, believe it or not).

Anyway, before I digress to much, let's get back on point. Aside from the spiritual definition of manifesting, the standard dictionary definition of it is "show (a quality or feeling) by one's acts or appearance; demonstrate." Note: that's simple, isn't it? It's about "DOING". I like doing words.... Good, old, verbs!

So, when it comes to The Art of Womanifesting, it's fundamentally about taking action, doing stuff, executing, making shit happen, grabbing life by the tits (that's my womanly replacement for balls) and havin' it! It's quitting dilly-dallying through life so we don't find ourselves on our death beds, riddled with resentment and regret. One of my favourite sayings is this:

 "Only regret the things you didn't do, never the things you did."

There's still more to it than this (Obvs, otherwise I'd never fill the next 150 pages!) The output of my work over the last few years spent studying other women (through my coaching practice, not in a stalker kinda way) and my own life experiences (I'll tell you some corking stories and give you all my juicy goss along the way) have given me the opportunity to distil everything I've learned (most often the hard way) into a methodology that makes it easy peasy, squeezy lemons for you! It's called The Woman Up Way and it looks a little something like this (well, this is ACTUALLY it):

At the heart of this process are the three mindsets I spoke about in the last section. Remember, they always come first because they underpin all of the changes we choose to make to ourselves, they allow us to set ourselves up for success in creating lasting, sustainable change. Once we've nailed that we can begin to work on the skill and behavioural layers. We always start with Identity. Why? Because it's super important to reconnect with your true identity and recognise the person that stares back at you when you look in the mirror. Without that, you're just playing the 'game face' game.

The epitome of a happy, fulfilled and successful woman is one who is secure, skilled and confident in each of the 7 elements of The Woman Up Way. That doesn't always mean you delve deeply into every area (on my programme, you get to complete a profiling questionnaire which shows you where your strengths and opportunities lie), you can easily dip in and out of the elements in order to support your own development needs and priorities. That means that you don't need to read the rest of this book in order. You can jump from chapter to chapter in whatever order you like. You're in the driving seat! I'm all about CHOICES and you have the freedom to choose. There is an AND to this though too. If you are feeling totally lost right now, don't recognise the women staring back at you in the mirror, lost your mojo entirely, feel flat as a pancake, got no oomph (I love that word, oomph), have no idea where to start because your life feels like one massive clusterfuck (also a fave word of mine), then I do highly recommend working through this one step at a time in the order I've mapped them out. There is a natural flow and build to them which will get you biggest bang for your buck, if you do decide to follow the process.

We're not done in this chapter just yet though. I know, I know, you're chomping at the bit to get going but hear me out on this one.... You want to do this once and do it right, yeah? You want to become that happy, fulfilled and successful woman in the fastest way possible, don't you? You want to take the path of least resistance? Of course, you do! Then turn the page and let me firstly share with you the plethora of common mistakes that women make (me included - I went through all the hard work so you don't have to, remember).

———

The Common Mistakes Women Make

Back in my corporate days, when I'd be working on the leadership solutions of large scale, behavioural transformation programmes, I learned a very valuable approach. An approach that is transferable from business and into every day life. That approach is defining the discreet behaviours that enable high performance and attempting to "bottle them", in order to replicate them by teaching them to other people. We called it "What Good Looks Like (WGLL)". I like this phrase:

 "Successful people are the ones who figure out what works and repeatedly do it."

BOOM! Job done right? Not quite. You see, through this approach, we'd also observe the behaviours of the lowest performers. What for? Because it's also useful to understand what drives the wrong or lower quality outcomes so that we can mitigate them or avoid them. And that's what I'd like to share with you here first. The seven chapters that follow will be sharing with you those "bottled" discreet behaviours that will help you to achieve the happy, fulfilling and successful live you bloody well deserve. But here, I'm sharing with you "What Good DOESN'T Look Like", so that you don't have to go through some of the painful lessons that I (and other women) have been through. We can just cut them out and take the detour!

Now, are you ready? It's a fairly long list so I'd recommend you get yourself a cuppa (or a glass of something lovely) and get comfy. In fact, whilst you're at it, get yourself a scribbling implement of some description and your most gorgeous note-book (I know you're a stationery magpie like me!) and I'd like you to clock up how many of these do or have applied to you. PS... It's not a contest and there are no prizes, coz remember, these ones are shit!

The Common Mistakes Woman Make (in complete random order coz that's how I roll - see Chapter 6 - Communication for explanation):

- They try to please all the people all the time;
- They don't put their own oxygen mask on first (see cabin crew safety briefing on a flight for more info);
- They fall into the comparison trap - They see other people's "snapshots" on Instagram, not the whole "movie";
- They bottle stuff up and end up bitter, twisted and resentful;
- They believe that they weren't born assertive therefore they never can be;
- They believe the life they dream of "doesn't happen to people like them" (one of my classics!);
- They're influenced too easily by other people's opinions;
- They self sabotage and get in their own way;
- They don't know what they want (but they know what they don't want);
- They're scared of having an opinion because of how others might judge them;

- They're too bothered about what other people think;
- They try to spin too many plates and spread themselves too thin, rendering themselves inefficient and ineffective (sorry, that one stings, doesn't it?);
- They struggle to articulate themselves;
- They have no personal boundaries or do, but don't uphold them and allow themselves to be violated by others (and yes, that can be as bad as it sounds);
- They allow themselves to be swamped with guilt for doing something 'nice' for themselves;
- They don't take care of themselves physically or mentally;
- They have low/no self-worth and/or self-respect;
- They have no purpose;
- They live out their lives through other people e.g., their kids;
- They live out other's old-fashioned expectations of them e.g., their parents;
- They give in or give up on things too easily and throw the towel in at the first hurdle;
- They have no influence or credibility and don't get taken seriously (usually because they don't value themselves and take themselves too seriously);
- They're scared of confrontation, conflict and challenge.

I could go on but I'll pause it there. How did you do? As a rough yardstick, if you got less than 5 then you are smashing it! Go give this book to your friend! You are a Womanifesting legend! If you got between 5 - 10 you're winning at life, whoop whoop! Between 10 -15 there's defo some value in you reading this book. 15+ I got you girl! You're in safe hands. Stick with me, work through this step by step, page by page, taking action as we go and we'll have you nailing it in a jiffy!

You deserve a refill after all that. See you in 5 over the page.

―――

Lessons from Hannah Montana

OK, bizarre title for a book section but hold on, let me explain. Depending on how old you are, this might ring some bells. One of my biggest lessons in life (and I mean BIGGEST) comes from Hannah Montana.

For those unfamiliar, Hannah Montana was a Disney series aired between 2006 - 2011 about a teenage girl called Miley Stewart (AKA Miley Cyrus) who had an alter ego, Hannah Montana, a world-famous pop star.

One of Hannah Montana's huge hit records was The Climb. I know, I know, you're sat there thinking, C'mon Jodes, seriously? So far, I thought you were a really cool, credible, woman and you're literally about to set fire to it. You were 30 years old in 2009 when the track was released! This is a bit sad.

But just let go of the 'Disneyness' (is that a word? It is now) of it for a moment. Forget who sang it. Just connect with the lyrics. To help you, I've summarised them below (because I'm not allowed to actually write them in here). If you don't know the song, I highly recommend you get on YouTube or Spotify right now, play it and listen carefully to the words. (I SO want you to post on your socials doing this and tag me in it!!!) More prizes!!!

The song describes how she visualises her dream, but her inner voice is telling her she'll never reach it. She feels lost and her faith starts to waiver. But she clings to the fact that she's got to keep trying and hold her head high. That's when she acknowledges something about herself that resonates so strongly with me too. That there's always going to be another mountain that she wants to move. It's going to be hard and actually, sometimes she won't be as successful as she hoped she would. However, her lightbulb moment is in realising that it's not about her getting there quickly or even the outcome or result in itself... it's all about the journey and how you grow along it.

Go press PLAY now. I'll see you in five.

OK, so if you've listened, you're now thinking "So what, Jodes? What the fuck was all that about?"

Well, as I said at the beginning of this section, this song gave me one of my greatest life lessons. I can't listen to this track without crying. EVERY. SINGLE. TIME. I'm one of those people, yeah, that's always chasing the next big dream. (This one wasn't in the list on the previous page and I think it should have been). I decide I want to achieve something, I set my mind to it, I make it happen, I get there. And I'm still not happy. Why? Because my brain hasn't even stopped to acknowledge the 'thing' that I've just delivered. It's already onto the next big thing. Stretching the art of the possible even more. Trying to get there UBER fast. "Impatient Annie" my mum always called me. And so, because they are the stories I've been telling myself for years, "I'm one of those people", then I am! Thing is, it doesn't make me feel happy, fulfilled or successful. Here's the liberating bit of where this song inspired me the most....

I get to CHOOSE my own story. I get to rewrite it whenever I feel like it. And I choose to rewrite it with this song. There is always gonna be another 'next big thing' and Yes, I'm always gonna want to smash it out of the park BUT, I now also choose to believe that it's absolutely ALL ABOUT THE JOURNEY!

We all know that corny, cheesy, quote....

 "Happiness is not a destination. It's a journey."

Well, never a truer word said. So, it's time to embark on the journey. Are you coming with me? Let's get started.

Now, I'm no Hannah Montana, but you are about to meet my alter ego... turn the page to meet Violet.

FOUR

IDENTITY

What Would Violet Do?

HOKEY COKEY! (That old chestnut again?) Let's get this show on the road!

It's time to begin to get under the bonnet on The Woman Up Way and that begins by exploring our Identity.

WHO THE FUCK ARE YOU? Like really? Who do you see when you look in the mirror? Who IS the person staring back at you?

If you're anything like me you've had more than one occasion in your life when you've looked in the mirror and not recognised the woman staring back. You don't know who you are anymore? You've lost touch with the person you used to be. You've lost your mojo. You feel like a nobody. Pretty insignificant. You're not alone. There are many more women feeling like this than you'd imagine but nobody dares say it out loud.

This has happened to me a few times. Most recently as I turned 40, a couple of years back. However, the most significant time was when I was just 27. I had settled down with my boyfriend that I'd been with since we were 15 at school. We'd had two children, girls aged three and one. We got married as that was what was expected of us. Then 7 months later I woke up one day, literally one day, looked in the mirror and thought "What am I doing?" "Who am I?" It filled me with panic. Long story short, I chose to walk away from my marriage. I got a lot of stick for that but I was never going to be that woman who "stayed for the kids". Here's why – kids aren't stupid. They can sense if they have a happy mum or not and I knew I could be a better mum if I made choices for myself. Plus, these children grow up and move out and leave you behind with a husband you can't stand. Then not only have you lived your life for your kids, they've left you behind and then your marriage falls apart.

I'm on a mission to help as many women as possible to avoid having that experience. I want to help women live their own lives by being confident and full of self-worth and self-esteem. And for me, there is just one simple, sure-fire way to make that happen – to reconnect with their true, authentic identity. Remember, I said simple, not easy.

So, you want to hear how I did it? Then I shall begin...

I was visiting my parents one afternoon and we were looking at old photos. I came across this one picture of me and I couldn't take my eyes of it. I was so unbelievably drawn into it. It was mesmerising. It reflected back to me the REAL me, the person who I was born to be. I knew her. I felt deeply connected to her. I could feel how she felt in that picture. And I wanted her back. This is that picture:

This is me. Age Four. In my favourite dress that I loved. I remember this so vividly. Yes, I remember the dress but here's what I remember more...

You only have to look at my face and my body language to see that I felt free. My most vivid memory about this moment is that I didn't have a care in the world. I had a zest for life! I was filled with joy. I was the pure and best version of me. I was the me without any fear, any limiting beliefs, any cares in the world. I could be and do anything I set my mind to, anything was possible and I had a wild imagination. I was invincible. I had massive dreams for myself and my life and believed that the world was my oyster. I was going to be an interpreter when I grew up, and travel the world.

As I grew older my dreams grew smaller – I was told by teachers...

> "Girls who dye their hair do not pass their exams."

At parents evening my French teacher told my parents:

> "She'll be lucky if she gets a D."

I overheard a comment once,

> "I bet she'll be pregnant before she is 16."

A boyfriend who told me:

> "You're nothing without me. I'll mould you into what you need to be."

My dad laughed and told me

> "You're deluded if you think you can pass your driving test after only 2 lessons and with your arm in plaster."

My point here is that I was surrounded by a society that were writing my story for me. It would be so easy to just follow the narrative, live <u>down</u> to that expectation and conform. To bury and let go of all that I wanted and desired for myself... but the thing is...**they picked the wrong girl!**

I've always had this fire in my belly, a deep sense of being a fighter, a non conformist, a rule breaker. In fact, this is my favourite quote of all time...

 "If you obey all the rules, you miss all the fun."

Here's what actually happened:

1. I ace'd my GCSE's – especially FRENCH.
2. At 16 I took off to Magaluf for the summer with my friends and I wasn't pregnant.
3. I married the boyfriend... and divorced him 10 months later.
4. I passed my driving test first time, with only 2 minor faults.

You see, here's what happens in reality. As we grow up, we're laden with expectations, societal norms, biases, prejudices, other people's beliefs and it weighs us down. We're taught to conform, be quiet, be a good girl, look pretty, act a certain way. All of that bullshit strips us of our inner beauty and dims our light so that by the time we're a young adult, we've lost all of that good stuff. We're conditioned to work hard, get a good job, settle down, get a mortgage, blah, blah, blah. We wear so many other 'badges' as I call them – we spend more time being 'wife', 'mum', 'HR manager', 'cleaner', 'carer' – you get the picture? We very rarely wear our own badge with our name on it. That's how we lose touch with our own self and why we end up not recognising the woman staring back.

So, these days, when I feel like this, I ask myself one simple but powerful question...

———

"What would Violet do?"

Oh, yes! I must explain. You see, in 1983 it really wasn't cool to be called Jodie. There weren't many of us around, so I used to tell people different names. I have been known to call myself Madonna and Charlotte amongst others, but my favourite of all time was Violet. And so, that picture you see is one of Violet. I go back to her and ask what she would do. That's always a very different answer than I would get from 42-year-old Jodes who has been tainted by society. When I step back into being Violet, I immediately become flooded with all of the confidence, self-worth, self-esteem, joy, imagination, excitement and belief that she had and it helps me to choose to behave differently, to break the mould, to do what I want, not what's expected of me. To put my desires, wants and needs front and centre.

So that's it. It's the one simple, sure-fire way to confidence, self-worth and self esteem (there is more, which I'll talk about further into this chapter but it's most certainly your first, best, step (thanks Rox)). Go back to the purest and best version of yourself. Find a picture of her and pin her up so that when you're stuck on the hamster wheel of life with the wrong badge on and you don't recognise the woman staring back at you in the mirror, you go to her and you ask her – what would she do?

PS.... I would love to connect with you on these. Please post them on social media and tag me in them. Pretty please xxx (Oh... use the hashtag #whatwouldvioletdo).

———

From Nobody to Somebody - the stories we tell ourselves and how to rewrite yours

Ever felt like a nobody? Shit innit?

You feel unnoticed. Insignificant. Pointless. A burden even. You look around you and see all of these 'somebodies' - being noticed, highly successful, in demand. But you're not like them, are you?

It's time to stop being Cinderella and never getting to go to the ball. It's time to change the way you see those "ugly sisters" and quit wishing you were like them. It's just a fairy tale anyway. A silly story.

But hang on a minute... What is your own life if it is not a story? And guess what? You get to hold the pen. The best bit... You get to write the next chapter.

I'm not sure where your head's at with this, but here's where mine is: I'm not into the notion that our life is mapped out for us. That what will be will be. That we waft through life on some pre-destined path that was mapped out for us. I think that's really crappy accountability. And you know how important accountability is in this whole Woman Up setup... yeah, it's flippin fundamental!

C'mon, ditch the victim mentality. Quit being 'done to'. If you find yourself saying things like....

"Nothing good ever happens to me";

"I'm just not a lucky person";

"Yeah but, I can't do that because... blah blah blah";

"It's so unfair";

"It's not my fault";

"Well, if X hadn't done blah blah blah";

"I'll just have to cross my fingers and hope it turns out ok";

... then they are big clues and red flags!

There's no big deal to moving from being a nobody to a some-body. You just choose to. You take accountability for your life, the choices and the decisions that you have made that have brought you to this point and you OWN THE SHIT out of what comes next! YOU are the author of this story. YOU get to decide how it pans out. YOU get to write the ending.

Now, I get it, right. There might have been some shit in your past that totes wasn't your fault. That put you in awful circum-stances. That subjected you to a whole host of appalling bull-shit. But please, PLEASE, don't tell yourself that that's you forever. That it is part of who you are, it's in you DNA, it's how you were made. That won't serve you, I guarantee it.

Instead, I want you to take accountability for becoming the person you WANT to be. Be a "Make Shit Happener". There's just four simple steps to achieving it too. It looks like this:

1. Acknowledge Reality - If you like a bit of Love Island it sounds like this "It is what it is, really."
2. Own It - Recognise that if you want something different for yourself, it's down to you, nobody else.
3. Find Solutions - There's more than one way to skin a cat, right? Come up with as many different hare-

brained ideas and ways to achieve the thing that you're after. Don't discount ANYTHING at this stage!

4. Make It Happen - This is where even the best people screw it up. YOU ACTUALLY HAVE TO DO SOMETHING! (Funny little story about that below*) You have to choose one of those solutions you came up with and DO IT. EXECUTE!

*Once, back in my corporate bullshit days, I was facilitating a workshop for some leaders. It was one of a series of sessions I was doing with them to help them to embed their learning and you know, take action. These sessions were 'accountability sessions' (the clue is in the title). I'd taught them the Ultimate Success Formula (I'll teach it to you later too, well, actually, no time like the present, is there?) which is this:

1. Know what you want.
2. Know why you want it.
3. Take massive action.
4. Review, tweak approach, rinse and repeat.

#simples, right?

I asked them to give me an update on their action plans that they'd written weeks before. They waffled on around the houses, talking a load of fluff basically, you know what it's like, when people have been talking for like 5 minutes and you've essentially learned sweet FA. Yeah, well, that's what it was like. They'd fannied around for the best part of a month and done naff all. So, I said to them, "OK, let's take a few steps back here to the Ultimate Success Formula. You knew what you wanted, you knew why you wanted it, but you've done FUCK ALL. You actually have to DO SOMETHING!"

(Sorry, that was really passive/aggressive of me - sarcasm, remember? - Hey, I never said I was perfect!)

So, the moral of the story is this... Only you get to decide who you are and it's down to you to make it happen. Not somebody else or some crappy circumstances.

Tell you what, here's a top tip. This is one that really propelled me forwards: When you've decided who you want to be, spend a little bit of time mapping out and bringing to life what that version of you would look like, sound like, do, be, what lifestyle you'd lead etc. Then rather than think "when I get there, I'll start being this person", step into that stuff TODAY. Start saying, doing, looking like, acting like that person NOW.

I learnt this from a business course I did with a lovely and amazing lady called Laura Phillips (@lauraphillipshq), the founder of Love to Launch™ who put it in much simpler terms... instead of HAVE - DO - BE, we BE - DO - HAVE.

(So, in the wise words of Missy Elliott... 'put your thang down, flip it and reverse it - for the record, that bit is me, not Laura Phillips. I'm not sure she'd thank me for that association.)

———

Limiting Beliefs

OK, so, you've got your head around the fact that it's important you take accountability for yourself. But is that enough? We're deep and meaningful creatures. There's a bit more to us than that. We're flippin complex fuckers. Some days I wish we weren't.

You'll likely have come across a phrase at some point in your life of 'limiting beliefs'. A limiting belief is a state of mind, conviction, or belief that you think to be true that limits you in some way. They prevent us from pursuing our goals, dreams and desires, therefore, they play a significant role in our Identity. They are just another form of the stories we tell ourselves, often holding us back from becoming that 'somebody' we dreamt of being.

We do it all day long: we tell ourselves a story about what's happening in our lives, about other people, about ourselves. When we call them "stories", that doesn't mean they're false, or that they aren't based on the truth. It just means we've constructed a narrative based on our experiences, a perspective on the world around us, an interpretation of facts as we see them. Not false, but not necessarily the entire truth - just one perspective. If you've ever gotten into the world of NLP (Neuro Linguistic Programming) you'll be familiar with the phrase 'your map of the world'. We each have a very different and unique one.

The law of the sod dictates that these stories we tell ourselves are, generally speaking, negative ones. They're rarely examples of how we're so brilliant. Hence why they become limiting beliefs. And the double whammy is that we've got a shed load of unconscious cognitive biases thrown into the mix just to distort reality even further! Triffic, as Del Boy from Only Fools and Horses would say.

Let's just take one. Confirmation bias. It means 'the tendency to process information by looking for, or interpreting, information that is consistent with one's existing beliefs'. So basically, whatever you believe to be true about yourself, or someone else, your brain goes looking for evidence to reinforce that belief. Why? Because human beings like to be right and this allows us to say to ourselves "See, I was right". But it gets worse... Not only does it actively go looking for evidence to support the shitty belief that doesn't serve us, it also makes a job out of filtering and discounting any positive evidence to the contrary. And conscious you doesn't even get a look in! Your brain gets rid of all this data before you've even clocked it, so you never knew it was ever there.

Limiting beliefs are weird things because of how they manifest. Like, we ACTUALLY say stuff to ourselves, don't we? Examples of mine....

"Why would anyone want to read a book that you've written?"

"OMG Jodie, you're such an imbecile".

"You can't wear dresses with legs like tree trunks".

They're an actual voice, aren't they? C'mon, don't make me look like the crazy lady, we've all got one, haven't we?

So, how do you shake off the limiting beliefs so that you can release yourself from their shackles and spread your wings of freedom? Good bloody question! It's taken me years to nail this one but I'm hoping I can assist you in a speedier time-frame. Here's what I found most useful. I read a book called 'Tame Your Gremlin', by Rick Carson. The most impactful part of this book for me was learning to detach from my inner voice. It is not me. I treat it like another being. In the book, it recommends giving your inner voice an Identity (yeah, I know we're working on your identity right now and this might be a bit confusing but your inner voice needs one too). That means deciding what it looks like and giving it a name. Here's my inner voice. Her name is Felicity and she's inspired by the Flanimals by Ricky Gervais. But designed by my lovely and very talented friend, Fi Woodhead (@fifi_designlady)

You've heard a few of the shitbag things she says to me above in those examples, but I made it my mission to get it all down on paper. List all the ways she tries to drag me down - I call this 'Noticing her Nonsense'. The other critical point I gleamed from the gremlin book was that it's not a wise move to engage in an argument with your inner voice, you're playing a losing game. That said, there is an alternative way to successfully handle the situation. I call it 'Choosing to Play'. This means toying about with some of the language to release it and make it more empowering. A really basic example:

The inner voice says to you "You can't do that."

I would choose to play with that by adding the word 'yet' e.g. "I can't do that, yet."

Bit further: "I've chosen not to do that."

Then I take it one step further: "I've chosen not to do that, until now."

I've now disarmed her. I've taken her power away because I've taken ownership of it. I'm now choosing. I'm making today the day that I can and will do it. As soon as I give my brain conscious evidence of the fact that I can do it, I start to form a new belief.

Scrapping old limiting beliefs and creating new ones that serve you is a straightforward (note I didn't say easy) process. I like to use an analogy to bring this one to life with my coaching clients. Imagine your brain is like a giant field of super tall sweetcorn. It's like a maze. Now, you go into this field everyday and you've created some pathways that allow you to get from once place to another (neural pathways). These are well trodden paths that you can now follow on autopilot, they're habitual. They're also your crappy limiting belief, thinking patterns. When it comes to creating new beliefs, it requires us to walk a brand-new path (form a new neural pathway), which involves treading down some of those tall sweetcorn plants. The first time we walk it we might make a barely noticeable path so next time we really have to concentrate and focus to see where we went. But, the more and more times we walk that new path, the more well trodden it becomes until its easy. And the added bonus? Whilst we've been busy creating our new path, our old one has become overgrown - result!

So, my challenge to you is to take some time out to do this task. You can easily do your own version of it, but if you'd like a template to help you then by all means head over to the Woman Up FREE resources section on my website HERE >>> bit.ly/woman-up-FREE-resources

———

Confidence, Self-Worth and Self-Esteem

Confidence.

I get really annoyed by the overuse and slapdash application of this word.

If I had a quid for every manager I'd heard tell one of their team members to "just work on being a bit more confident" I'd be a flippin billionaire by now! Maybe you've had it said to you? Possibly in a friendship capacity, not even work? Maybe it's you that has said it to other people... "C'mon, just be a bit more confident"

Incoming Passive Aggressive alert - Well, yeah right! Why didn't I think of that? What a silly thing to say to someone. Sadly, we weren't born with a magic little switch on our backs that we could just flick on when we needed a bit of a confidence boost, nor can we just pop some in our trolley whilst doing the online grocery order - if only it were that easy!

Most of us lack confidence in at least some situations. For some people, they feel like the confidence tank is permanently running on empty. Some believe in the mantra "fake it till you make it" - utter bollocks if you ask me! I can smell it a mile off and it reeks of inauthenticity. But it's an essential ingredient if you're gonna carry off this nifty, newfound identity of yours with some degree of swagger. So, let's strip this one back a bit and get down into the nooks and crannies of it all so we know what we're on about, what we're really after and how to go about genuinely knocking it out of the park.

Let's begin by gaining some clarity on the definition of a few things. You'll see this section of this chapter is called 'Confidence, Self-Worth and Self- Esteem'. Most people use these words interchangeably to describe the same things, but they are actually all quite different.

Confidence - Self-confidence is how much you truly believe in yourself and what you can do.

Self worth - Self-worth is your deeply held feeling about your own value as a person.

Self esteem - Self-esteem is the way you feel about yourself in different areas, like intelligence, personality, appearance, and success.

So, confidence is a more over-arching concept about how much you believe in yourself and what you're capable of in a broad sense. Self-worth and self-esteem are more specific about exploring to what degree we value ourselves and how we 'feel' about ourselves in different situations. I think it's important to get these terms straight in our minds. Why? Not because I'm a pedantic, nit-picking knob head, but because this clarity better helps us to figure out the HOW in terms of growing our confidence. My issue with most developmental actions on a PDP is that they always talk about the WHAT but rarely help anyone out with the HOW. And if we don't know how, then we haven't got a cat in hells chance of improving it.

It's clear to see, now we've cleared that up, that to be more confident (and therefore be comfortable in the skin of our true Identity), the job to be done is on our self-worth and self-esteem - how much we believe we're worth it and how we really feel about ourselves in different situations and circumstances.

While we're here and at it, we might as well chuck a bit of self-awareness into the mix, too. A good dollop of that sorts all kinds of discombobulation out!

Self-awareness - how well you know your own abilities, talents, capabilities, preferences, likes and dislikes, wants and needs.

OK, let's not run before we can walk... at this point, it's worthwhile just running through how each of these things can hold you back as that might give you something more recognisable to attach yourself to and resonate more strongly with you. Otherwise, we run the risk of you washing over it thinking you've got all this crack down and skipping on to the next chapter. If you don't address it now, in the foundation, you'll come a cropper further down the line so, top tip... Do the work anyway.

- Self-confidence: Having low self-confidence makes it hard to try new things or reach for new challenges. Anxiety is a natural result that holds you back and you'll find that you like to stay in your comfort zone.
- Self-worth: Low self-worth undermines what you are willing to do for yourself. Are you worthy of another person's attention and love? Are you deserving of receiving good things? Do you have enough to offer other people so that they might value you? Having low self-worth prevents you from believing in yourself and from claiming what is yours.

- Self-esteem: When you have low self-esteem, you walk through the world in a one-down position. You operate from a place of 'I'm not good enough'. Everything that happens in your life is filtered through that deeply held notion, even though it is definitely not true. So even mundane interactions, once they go through your filter, can end up hurting you.
- Self-awareness: How well, and how accurately, do you see yourself? Can you predict how you will act, or how you will feel, in certain situations? Are you aware of your own strengths and preferences? Low self-awareness makes it hard to make good choices for yourself, and hard to believe in the decisions you make.

Any of those ring true for you? OK, so what do you do about it? HOW do you build up to being more confident so you can live in that fabulous identity you've just rediscovered? Now, we could spend a week-long course doing the graft on this - my programme teaches you loads more (hint, hint) - but here's a bunch of easy and simple top tips to get you started:

1. Start with self-awareness. Become more present with yourself. Notice YOU more. Journal about your reflections, thoughts and feelings and see what it shows up for you. When you feel triggered by something (negatively or positively), pause and ask yourself the questions "Ooh, what's that all about then?" (It has to start with the "ooh" btw. Ha!)
2. You may be someone who, without realising it, doesn't acknowledge emotions and therefore you neglect

yourself emotionally. A lot of people find it extremely difficult - in fact, there're not even proactively conscious of it - to know what emotion they're feeling. Practice labelling your feelings when you experience them and sit with them for a while.

3. Start to seek your validation of yourself internally rather than externally. I was a MASSIVE external validator when I started this journey. I was in constant need of hearing it from somebody else of whether I was any good or not. Over time, I've slowly transitioned that to push myself to make the decision myself of whether I was any good or not and either letting go of, or not even seeking the opinions of anyone else.

4. Drop the judgement - we live in a very judgey world these days (I'll harp on about this loads throughout this book, get used to it). We judge other people so much that we're all super bothered now about what everyone else is thinking. But the worst thing? We're far more judgey than we realise of ourselves. Try letting go of drawing meaning from a situation. Leave it be. Observe it simply for what it is. Resist the temptation to decide if it was good or bad, right or wrong, pretty or ugly... whatever.

Get cracking with these small steps to begin with. I'm a huge believer in small change, big difference. You don't have to turn yourself upside down, inside out and back to front to sort your life out. Making small, positive tweaks is all it takes to revolutionise your life! Give 'em a whirl and let's see you shining like a diamond in that new found confidence of yours!

Self-Sabotage

Uh! I almost hate to write this section of this chapter but it's pretty damn important. I get super cross that there is such a thing in the world as self-sabotage. Who came up with this daft notion? Some flippin goon I tell you!

Self-sabotage is when we actively or passively take steps to prevent ourselves from reaching our goals - why on earth would we do that? But we do. I couldn't see it in myself for YEARS and then I had a big, breakthrough Ah-ha moment. (Anyone else singing "Take on me" now?... sorry.)

Ok, so it's annoying bullshit but why does it happen? Turns out it's often a learnt behaviour that served us or soothed us in an earlier traumatic or tricky experience. We form patterns out of them in early life and they naturally become our autopilot. They mean something to us and they're hard to give up - bit like smoking.

Where does it tend to show up? Have a goosey gander at the list and see how many of these strike a chord with you:

- Blaming other people when things go wrong.
- Throwing the towel in and walking away if things don't go smoothly.
- Procrastination - oh hello!
- Picking fights and arguments with friends, family or partners.
- Constantly dating gaslighting dickheads!
- Trouble articulating your needs and wants.
- Not setting and upholding personal boundaries.

- Putting yourself down.
- Being a martyr.
- Fear of failure.
- A need for control.

I'm pretty sure this list is not exhaustive so feel free to add your own (although, as before, your don't get points for having more).

It was only when I broke it down to this level that I was able to see my behaviour for what it really was. My top 3 are: Fear of failure (I hide when I'm scared of it not working); procrastination (I'm a gold medalist at putting things off); Throwing the towel in (I hate myself for this one but it's true).

Only when you've identified these things can you do something about them. I'm going to speak from experience on this one and share with you my pitfalls to avoid and my quick wins to get you motoring along towards the good stuff again.

1. Find someone who will call you out on your bullshit. This is when you need a highly trusted friend who you know has your back and will be really frank and honest with you, but come from a really good place. I like to call these 'accountability buddies'.
2. Learn what your triggers are so you can head them off in advance. Most of us, if given the time, can spot patterns of self-sabotage in our behaviour. Knowing these upfront and the warning signs can mean you can head it off before it becomes an issue.
3. If you're like me and have a massive fear of failure (plus extremely high standards), I recommend... wait

for it... Start failing and failing fast. Shift your mindset to one of "the quickest way to learn and get better is by making mistakes". Make mistakes ok for you. Then go back to my earlier point of not drawing meaning from that mistake. It is what it is. What does it teach you? Move the fuck on.

Self-sabotage can really become a show stopper if you let it. Most of us would be so happy, fulfilled and successful if we juts got out of our own way! If you're recognising that self-sabotage is a bit of a blocker for you, then I highly recommend you go check out my absolute legend of a friend and all-round right bobbydazzler of a chick, Dani Wallace - you'll find her on socials as The Queen Bee (on the gram she is @thequeen-beedani). She is epic at all things self-sabotage.

———

How to be the Best and Most Authentic Version of You

Authenticity has become a bit of a buzz word lately, hasn't it? Whether that's in corporate crapology, the online entrepreneurial space or with celebs. The irony is that most who harp on about it are actually the most inauthentic people!

Being the best and most authentic version of you is so significantly hung from being connected to your true identity. It's like a tree having really deep roots. It really grounds you, gives you unwavering stability and allows you to feel immensely secure.

What does it mean though? Well, authentic is just a fancy word for genuine. Genuine simply means that you are what you say you are - the real deal. Best version of yourself? Tony Robbins defines it as this:

 "Becoming the best version of yourself means getting back to your quintessential self. As straightforward as that sounds, it's anything but: Authentic self-discovery takes courage and tenacity. To approach your essential self, you must turn away from distracting false beliefs that cloud or distort your self-perception."

Now, we've spent a bit of time already taking a look at those distracting false beliefs and the distortions. We've touched briefly on courage when we defined what assertiveness really is. More on that later in the book, as well as getting under the skin on tenacity (that's a tough chapter... need to build you up to that one!)

For me, being the best version of myself is a decision. It's a decision to let go of all the expectations, criticism, self-doubt, negativity etc. It's about letting go, getting in flow. Following your heart, not just your head. It means being a constant work in progress and that requires a growth mindset (not a fixed one), never being the finished article (even though best self might sound like one). It's about living true to your values and your principles.

For many years I was ANYTHING BUT the best and most authentic version of me! I spent my life trying to 'fit in', to be accepted and have a sense of belonging. In God's honest truth, I cannot categorically say that I'm 100% my best and most authentic self every single day. Some people would say that is unrealistic anyway. However, I'd like to believe that it is absolutely possible (well, Violet says so anyway) and achievable and therefore I'm continuing to strive for it.

I'm just going to drop back to the 'self-worth' word for a mo. You see, fundamentally, as human beings, we're all driven by a sense of self-worth. Every action we take and behaviour we display is ultimately a quest to feel good about ourselves. It's just that sometimes, it all goes a bit Pete Tong and we get things a bit wonky in our application. Yes, we all know a few arseholes and twats but I still believe that deep down all they're trying to do is get back to a place where they have a sense of self-worth. And I also believe that we all deserve to have that. So next time you come across someone being a dick, just remind yourself that the situation has probably got a bit out of hand for them, they're out of their depth and they're just trying to claw back to a good place, but that's difficult when you're drowning. Throw them a life line.

If this is true of others that we encounter, then you can bet your bottom dollar that its true for you too. I'm gonna carry on running with the drowning analogy on this one to share with you how best to handle the situation... During the first wave of the Coronavirus pandemic in 2020, when the summer came round and the restrictions were lifted somewhat, we had a little day out in New Brighton on the Wirral coastline, not too far from where we live. Because the situation was still pretty dire, there were no lifeguards on the beach. Instead, there was a banner strapped to the railings that gave you some handy hints for if you got into difficulty in the water. They were pretty good suggestions actually, and not just for in the water. One of the tips was, instead of thrashing about in the water if you were struggling and fighting to keep your head above water, you should lie back, relax, make a star formation out of your body and float. The same can be said when we get into sticky wicket situations from a self-worth perspective. Instead of fighting against it, relax, lean into it, float and you will return to a state of safety and calm much quicker.

I notice that this strategy works best for me when I realise when I'm wrong. Previously I would front it out. Argue the toss. Not let go. This just made me look a plonker to be fair. Nowadays (ooh, I sound like a right old codger saying that!), I'm my best and most authentic self when I own up to getting something wrong. I admit if I've made a booboo. I put my hand up and say sorry, that was me! And do you know what? I gain so much more credibility and respect as a result. Plus, it's a lot less stressful.

So, how can you be the best and most authentic version of yourself? Here's some thoughts...

- Work out your why - have purpose and meaning in the life you live, for yourself, not through other people (including your kids!)
- Use "System 2" thinking. According to Professor Daniel Kahneman, author of 'Thinking, Fast and Slow', System 2 is a way of thinking that is slow, deliberate, and thoughtful. It is used when making tough decisions or thinking "out of the box." It is opposite from System 1, which is dictated by automatic and fast ways of thinking. When we use the System 2 part of our brain, we instantly become more creative and challenge old ways of thinking.
- Avoid the Nocebo - A nocebo is a believed negative effect from an expectation about us. The expectation can come from ourselves or from others around us. Nocebo is a term coined in 1961 by Walter Kennedy, which in Latin means "I will harm". It's basically like a negative placebo effect. Instead have positive expectations about yourself and it will increase your likelihood of success.
- Quit with the excusitis - Yep. I've just invented a new medical condition. It's where you just keep coming up with bullshit excuses for stuff. Just knock it on the head and take accountability for yourself.
- Aim for being great, rather than perfect - ask yourself this question at the end of every day and if the answer is Yes, then sleep soundly... Did I do my best today? (Another Roxyism that's brilliant!)

––––––

Comparison is the Thief of Joy:

 "Comparison is the thief of joy."

- THEODORE ROOSEVELT.

One of my fave quotes of all time. There's not really much else to say, except, jack it in. It makes you feel like shit. Do something more serving for yourself. Oh... and if you must compare yourself to others, here's a couple of top tips.

1. Get the fuck off Instagram.
2. List the top 10 people that you rate at the thing you're comparing yourself on and then compare yourself to number 7 on that list, rather than number 1. It will give you a much more unbiased view.
3. If you must compare yourself, use it as a way to uncover the characteristics that you could emulate to improve yourself e.g., someone who's a better cook (shit example I know, it's late here) - Do they attend classes? Do they sharpen their knives regularly? Do they buy only local produce? Etc. Then do that stuff.

Finito.

FIVE

POWER

What is Power and Why Do We Want/Need It?

OK, so, Identity, tick. The next element of The Woman Up Way is Power. Your first immediate thought is "what's all this about then?"

Let's start with a question actually. Does the word power bring about positive or negative connotations for you? The majority of women I ask about this say negative. The majority of men however, say positive. That' a really interesting paradigm comparison but sadly, it's not that surprising.

Let's take the dictionary definition of power firstly (you can probably tell by now; I like a good definition to give us real clarity before we delve into something - people have some very weird and wonky definitions). As a noun, power means the ability or capacity to do something, or act in a particular way, or to direct or influence the behaviour of others or the course of events. So, if we go back to what Woman Up means then this is a great thing for women to possess right? The wonky version is that of coercion, pressure, manipulation, force, control. I'm super keen that we create a feminine version of power that is empowering and supports equality.

Why?

You've probably called yourself a control freak at some point in your life. Maybe not over everything, but over certain things. A desire for control stems primarily from feeling insecure and unsafe. It's our bodies way of protecting ourselves. The bottom layer of self-worth (which if you remember from the last chapter, is the quest we're all chasing in life) is self-preservation. When the chips are down, you feel like you've exhausted all of your options, your back is up against the wall and you've got nowhere to go, we head into self-preservation mode. That can play out for us in some weird behaviours that don't seem obvious. Some of the most "perceived" powerful people in the world grew up through a childhood of neglect and surrounded by emotional abuse, hence their control freak nature (think Christian Grey from Fifty Shades... you're welcome!). It's also worth taking a glance at your human needs. Our human needs, as defined by Tony Robbins, boil down to just six basic human needs that make us tick and drive our behaviour:

Need 1: Certainty/Comfort.

The first human need is the need for Certainty. It's our need to feel in control and to know what's coming next so we can feel secure. It's the need for basic comfort, the need to avoid pain and stress, and also to create pleasure. Our need for certainty is a survival mechanism. It affects how much risk we're willing to take in life - in our jobs, in our investments, and in our relationships. The higher the need for certainty, the less risk you'll be willing to take or emotionally bear. By the way, this is where your real "risk tolerance" comes from.

Need 2: Uncertainty/Variety.

Are you someone who gets bored easily? Hates routine? Needs a bit of spontaneity and excitement in life? If yes, you likely have a high need for uncertainty/variety. Mundane life gets you down. You thrive off some spark, a few surprises. Love a challenge to solve too. Happy to take the odd 'gamble' here and there.

Need 3: Significance.

We all need to feel important, special, unique, or needed. So how do some of us get significance? You can get it by earning megabucks, or collecting qualifications and badges - distinguishing yourself with a master's or a PhD. You can build a giant Instagram following. Some do it by putting tattoos and piercings all over themselves and in places we don't want to know about. You can get significance by having more or bigger problems than anybody else - "You think you've got it tough, try living my life for a day!" Of course, you can also get it by being more spiritual (or pretending to be).

Spending a lot of money can make you feel significant, and so can spending very little. We all know people who constantly brag about their bargains, or who feel special because they heat their homes with cow manure and sunlight.

Need 4: Love & Connection.

The fourth basic need is Love and Connection. Love is the oxygen of life; it's what we all want and need most. When we love completely, we feel alive, but when we lose love, the pain is so great that most people settle on connection, the crumbs of love. You can get that sense of connection or love through intimacy, or friendship, or prayer, or walking in nature. If nothing else works, you can get a dog.

These first four needs are what Tony calls the needs of the personality. We all find ways to meet these - whether by working harder, coming up with a big problem, or creating stories to rationalise them. The last two are the needs of the spirit. These are rarer - not everyone meets these. When these needs are met, we truly feel fulfilled.

Need 5: Growth.

If you're not growing, you're dying. If a relationship is not growing, if a business is not growing, if you're not growing, it doesn't matter how much money you have in the bank, how many friends you have, how many people love you - you're not going to experience real fulfilment. And the reason we grow, is so we have something of value to give.

Need 6: Contribution.

Corny as it may sound, the secret to living is giving. Life's not about me; it's about we. Think about it, what's the first thing you do when you get good or exciting news? You call somebody you love and share it. Sharing enhances everything you experience.

Life is really about creating meaning. And meaning does not come from what you get, it comes from what you give. Ultimately, it's not what you get that will make you happy long term, but rather who you become and what you contribute.

We'll dip in and out of some of these throughout the book, but for now, back in the room with Power - how is this relevant? Specifically, when it comes to power, the need for certainty / security and the need for significance take up a lot of power. What most people find when they look at all six of these needs is that there are usually a couple that are more at play for you than the others. This can change over time depending on what's going on for you. Mine, for example, are top of the shop - Uncertainty / Variety with a closely followed second of Significance. Here's the gig with these though. It's all about self-awareness. Knowing what your biggest needs are at any given time is important. Why? Because we find a way to meet them regardless of whether we do it consciously or not. When we do it consciously, we're able to meet them in a healthy way. When we do it sub-consciously there is a greater risk of meeting that need unhealthily.

Example: With my top two, meeting them healthily would look like proactively planning exciting fun times, adventures, meeting different people. It might also look like never going to the same place twice on holiday or always having something different for dinner (not always the same menu each week). However, if I ignore this need, I will end up meeting it unhealthily, for example, spending money online buying new clothes I don't need or can't afford, or going out drinking on a Tuesday night. With the need for significance, when meeting it healthily, I would study for a new qualification and add a new string to my bow or write this book! If I was meeting it unhealthily, I might turn into a gossip or be one of those annoying name-dropping type of people. Make sense? You can easily see there, with significance, how it can manifest itself for good and bad when it comes to power.

Power in a Woman Up context, the feminine version of power looks like this:

- Leveraging personal power rather than positional power.
- Being able to get out of your own way.
- Knowing what you want (not what you don't want).
- Behaving assertively.
- Have the ability to say No without feeling guilty.
- Tapping into your vulnerability and being ok with sharing it.
- Setting and maintaining personal boundaries.
- Letting go of judgement.
- Collaborating not competing.
- No longer giving a fuck what anyone else thinks.
- No allowing anyone or anything to intimidate you.

You'll be pleased to hear that these are the things that this chapter addresses! So, let's get cracking!

———

Personal vs Positional Power

For many women, they have mostly experienced being on the receiving end of positional power throughout their life, whether that be in a work context, a family context or a relationship context. Positional power is all about hierarchy. I'm throwing my hat into the ring right upfront on this one and stating I do not care one iota for positional power. Hierarchy means sweet FA to me. It's utter bullshit in this day and age.

Positional power is driven out of authority, rank, assets etc. It's an "I'm higher, more senior, got more cash, male, my own office and PA, older, than you." That just doesn't wash with me. Not only because it puts women closer to the bottom of the pile but, just as importantly, because it's wrong.

Cue, Personal Power. Personal power is about influence. It's driven out of doing the right thing, doing things right, contributing to the greater good, respect, credibility, trust. I sure as damn it would rather have those things than the former. Personal Power isn't autocratic. There's no JFDI in sight! It's like magic. It's magnetic. It compels people to come to you, to want to be on your team, to support you to drive your agenda, to achieve your goals - whether this be in a home or work scenario.

Now, it's easier said than done because it requires lashing and lashings of skill. Positional power is a piece of piss. You just holler at people to just fucking do it because I said. Any old crank can do that providing they've got the badge or the plaque on the door. Personal power is a skilful act. It requires you to have real presence (we'll cover that later), to genuinely care, to be assertive, to have the ability to influence, make bold but right decisions, be ethical, have strong principles and values, value diversity (not surround yourself with clones of yourself). But just because it's hard, doesn't mean we shouldn't do it. In fact, it adds more weight as to why we should. If we want to be respected by our partners, show our daughters and sons how to grow up into good people, lead our teams, accelerate our careers, make more money in our businesses, then it's worth it.

———

Getting Out of Your Own Way

Your own power requires stepping into.

We often view power in relation to something external from us rather than something within us. More often than not, what is holding us back, keeping us small, limiting our full potential is not someone else, but ourselves.

 "No one saves us but ourselves. No one can and no one may. We ourselves must walk the path."

BUDDHA

You may have settled for sitting on the side-lines instead of getting involved in the game of life with passion, purpose, and power.

It is no secret those who lead a fulfilling life have the power to create their own circumstances, owing to their enthusiasm and passion.

Let's go back to the brain...

We entertain anywhere between 70,000–80,000 thoughts a day. Most of those thoughts are repetitive and negative in nature. We worry about shit... A lot! (Have you noticed that most of the things we worry about never actually happen?) Then we tend to 'feel' our 'thoughts' - does that make sense? It's actually really fucking unhelpful. One of the most challenging and useful things I have EVER learned is that thoughts are just thoughts. Let them come, and let them go again. But hey-ho, let's roll with the fact that we end up with all of these feelings and emotions, some of which are quite frankly, really yucky to sit with. We'd rather chew our own fingers off that sit with them quietly.

In order to step into your powerful self, learn to face and embrace your feelings and emotions rather than become a victim of their erratic nature.

We know that situations in life can be shit. What you do with these feelings can be a showstopper as it relates to moving forward or staying stuck internally.

Many people do not like to feel pain, so they stuff down and bury their pain as they encounter it or try to numb it with addictions and stuff. I speak from experience here. 15 years ago, when I split up from my first husband and was living in a flat with my two girls whilst still paying the mortgage on the marital home and trying to hold down a full time job, I turned to codeine to cope. I had a constant headache that was all tension and stress, and paracetamol just didn't touch the sides. Before long, I was relying on co-codamol to get to sleep every night and within just a couple of weeks, couldn't get to sleep without it. It was a very slippery slope that I slid down for about six months, before acknowledging that there was an issue that I needed to deal with. Let's just say that was pretty unpleasant.

The effects of these rubbish coping skills drains us of all our energy over time, perhaps leading to an emotional breakdown at some point in some cases. If I can help to stop you from getting there, I'd really like to.

So, what I'm saying is, lean into those emotions and feelings. We do this by firstly knowing what emotion we're actually experiencing and naming it. You'd be surprised, not many people can do this. They know it doesn't feel nice but they put an umbrella emotion on it, a really broad one like "I'm angry" or "I'm upset" when actually, if you really peel back the layers, what you discover is that it's more than that. It's things like, embarrassment, humiliation, shame, jealousy, resentment, helplessness, abandonment, deep fear. I find it most helpful when I experience an emotion to first pinpoint where in my body I feel the sensation as well as describe what the sensation is e.g., it's in my head and it feels woozy or fizzy when I'm worried. It's in my chest and it feels flappy when it's anxiety. It's in my tummy and it's like butterflies when it's excitement/nervousness. Then I find it easier to label the emotion and I learn to recognise them easier/quicker next time. Once I've clocked it, I don't judge or berate myself for what I'm feeling. I get curious with it by asking myself "What's all that about then?" (A fabulous self-coaching question I learned from the wisdom of my amazing, good friend, Lynn Parker, aka Lady P). I sit with that question for a while and notice what comes up for me and I never accept my first or second response. Only when I get to my third do I sense that I'm really getting somewhere, that I'm deep enough. Finally, I go back to a technique my therapist taught me and that is to speak to my child self (Violet) as my adult self. What would I say to her? I'd be kind and compassionate. I'd encourage her. I'd boost her confidence and belief in herself. I'd tell her to go for it! That's when I reclaim my power and I get out of my own way. Try it for yourself.

What You Want, Not What You Don't Want

Tell me what you want, what you really, really want.

Yes, I know! Your head is now populated with a really annoying Spice Girls track! #sorrynotsorry

Short and sweet one this, but mightily important - PLESE DO NOT SKIP THIS ONE.

When I'm coaching women, one of the first questions I ask is "What is it that you want for yourself?" And I get met with one of two responses (I wonder which one you would be?):

1. They proceed to describe in detail everything that they DON'T WANT.
2. They say "I don't know. I've never really given it much thought."

What were you? 1 or 2?

I'm on a mission to get more women to be able to clearly articulate what they want for themselves.

A little story about me. In my first marriage, I put up with some crap. Was it his fault? No, not really. He never treated me well but I always believed I'd change him #schoolgirlerror. He was a big drinker and was always out with the lads, sinking 10 pints then coming home a bit lairy, cooking all kinds, nearly setting fire to the kitchen and then being sick on the floor before passing out. Now, I was no shrinking violet, let me tell you. But I'd constantly kick off about everything I hated and what I didn't want anymore. The turning point happened for

me one day when he got up with a hangover. I was having a
go about the night before and he was sat on the sofa with our
two girls (aged 4 and 2 at the time) under each arm and said to
them both "Look at your miserable, moody mum". It broke me.
It was at that point that I knew I had to step into my own
power and make some positive choices for myself. I also
needed to be a role model to my girls and show them what it
meant to be a strong, independent woman. He was a male
chauvinist, always had been. Quite openly a 'treat 'em mean,
keep 'em keen' kinda guy. It was time to decide what I
WANTED for MYSELF and go out and get it. That wasn't easy.
In fact, it was really, fucking, tough! Every time I tried to visu-
alise for myself what I wanted, it would come out as the opposite e.g. I don't want to be unhappy forever. I don't want to be
in an unhappy relationship. If I ever got close to saying what I
wanted it would twist halfway through the sentence like this...
I want to get away from this town. Don't be fooled by this! Just
because the sentence starts with "I want" doesn't mean it's
articulating what you actually want. It still describes what I
didn't want. Here's the trick... it requires you to get out of an
"away" mindset and more into a "towards" mindset. Can you
see how I was trying to get away from something? To be a true
want it would have sounded something like this "I want to go
back to the village where I grew up" or "I want to move to
Australia" - get the picture?

You see, how are you EVER going to get it if you can't speak
it? Either you've never figured it out and are wafting along
through life, aimlessly hoping something might just jump out
and grab you at some point, or you're one of those moaning,
nagging, life blood sucking women that are always, frickin

complaining about something, like I was. Yes, you know who you are! Not only does this make for a very unhappy existence, it's brings every fucker else around you down with you. You're the opposite of a magnet. You repel those you love and care deeply about away from you.

I'd like to you pause and take some time out at this point to reflect on what it is that you want for yourself (Oh, and if you're a mum, don't get sucked into the kid's trap. I don't want you living your life through them. This is about what YOU want for YOURSELF, not anybody else. And that doesn't mean you don't love them or don't care. You already know and deliver for them but you put yourself on the scrap pile. Time to budge yourself up the pecking order). Write it down. Get it out of your head. Say it out loud to yourself. And if you're brave go and declare it to the world by telling someone else or even posting it online and tagging me in it. I promise I'll be your biggest cheerleader!

———

Doormat, Diva or Alpha Female Bitch From Hell?

You probably immediately associated yourself with one of the above. It's also likely other people flew into your head too.

These are often terms used to describe many women when it comes to the assertiveness spectrum. At one end, the doormat, people pleaser, very passive person. At the other, the alpha female bitch from hell - the bossy and demanding woman, the aggressive person. The diva is an interesting one. Many people take pride in being labelled a diva but in the assertive stakes, it's not a compliment or a pleasant or attractive quality. A Diva being defined as a self-important person who is temperamental and difficult to please. Someone that is acting as entitled or holier than thou. A spoilt woman who wants things her own way and bosses people around.

For me, this is all about Power.

And it's an important element when it comes to how you 'Woman Up'.

The doormats and people pleasers lack power. The divas and the AFBFH let power go to their heads and it's the wrong kind of power - that positional power we spoke about.

Here's a common situation. Women in the workplace, particularly those who are in the mid to senior management and leadership roles, find themselves working in a predominantly male peer group. Often, there aren't many female role models to emulate. What frequently happens is women make an effort to try to 'fit in' by behaving like the men. This creates the classic

'Alpha Female Bitch from Hell' – most of us have experienced a version of this at some point in our career.

She gets labelled as 'bossy' and she passes that off as 'they can't handle an assertive woman', but in reality, she is aggressive (see illustration below). Now, that's not to say that the male behaviour is necessarily wrong (although sometimes it is extremely dysfunctional and toxic), but it doesn't wear well on a woman. Assertive behaviour looks and sounds different on different people, regardless of gender to some extent. In most cases, none of what is demonstrated is assertive.

To the women called "aggressive",
keep on being *assertive*

To the women called "bossy",
keep on *leading*

To the women called "difficult",
keep on *telling the truth*

To the women called "too much",
keep *taking up space*

To the women called "awkward",
keep *asking tough questions*

Be careful with these quotes above. I see things like this on social media all the time. Being called bossy doesn't necessarily mean you are leading. Being called difficult doesn't mean you are simply telling the truth. Being called too much doesn't mean you're owning your space and being called awkward doesn't mean you're just asking tough questions. Maybe you are aggressive, bossy, difficult, too much and awkward. That stuff is not being assertive.

At the other end of the spectrum, there's a rather large proportion of women who are passive in their approach.

By their own definition, the people pleasers and doormats; the peacekeepers and harmony crafters. They would rather 'suck it up' than 'upset the apple cart'. They really struggle to speak up and make their contribution (even though that contribution is worth its weight in gold) for fear of upsetting anyone or not being liked. These women are so troubled by what other people think of them its debilitating and paralysing. It's a pattern that has been ingrained in them since childhood – girls should be quiet and look pretty, be agreeable and 'nice', don't make a fuss etc.

This makes it very difficult to break away from, but it doesn't render it anywhere near impossible. It might involve some hard work, but that's ok, we can do hard stuff, especially when it's worth it!

Then there's the passive aggressive behaviour. Very few people identify this in themselves but it is very common. If you find yourself being sarcastic, flippant, apathetic, cynical, huffing and puffing whilst saying "I'm fine", muttering under your breath, giving someone the silent treatment or sulking, these are all examples of behaving in a passive aggressive way. Because this behaviour is both low in consideration and courage, it's the least favourable of all – it's on par with lose/lose thinking.

The assertive people with personal power don't need to shout their demands and they rarely make people feel inadequate or unappreciated. They have a way of being comfortable in their own skin, believing what they believe, and confidently saying their own opinions while being able to respect and honour others without feeling threatened.

So, it's plain to see how personal power lends itself to being truly assertive. As a reminder, assertiveness is the careful blend of consideration and courage – the ability to first listen to understand and work hard to satisfy the wants and needs of someone else. Then secondly, have the courage to state your own wants and needs and request that they be met too.

The assertive bill of rights really helps to demonstrate what this might look like in terms of mindset and behaviours - go back to it in Chapter 3 for a reminder if you need to.

If this has struck a chord with you, either as a people pleaser with zero power, or a diva with overplayed positional power, and you'd like to make some adjustments and move into the personal power space - to 'Woman Up!' - then here's my top tips:

1. Lighten up, ffs! (And have some fun.)
2. Learn to REALLY listen (to solely understand, not to prepare your next response).
3. Have bouncebackability – this is about resilience, tenacity, perseverance and grit (more of which I'll help you with in later chapters). Don't throw the towel in at the first hurdle or sign of it getting a bit hard or tricky.

When you embrace your personal power, it will likely have an impact on:

- Your work;
- Your personal life;
- Your goals;
- Your friends;
- Your business colleagues;
- Your happiness;
- Your health.

When you find your personal power, own it.

———

Guilt and The Guilt Free Formula for Saying No.

Hands up if you feel pangs of guilt on a daily basis?

Guilt robs us of our power; therefore, it's not welcome here. Time to nip it in the bud.

Women are riddled with guilt and in my book, it's got to change! I think we just accept it as par for the course and I'm not cool with that anymore.

Here's the most ironic thing of the century - Who feels guilty for feeling guilty? What a fucking joke that is!

Guilt is an emotion. So, think back to those emotions we were talking about earlier when we were getting out of our own way. Now you can add this one into the mix too! Joy, oh joy! Where do you experience guilt in your body? I experience it in my cheeks, believe it or not. When I feel bad for not doing something for someone else, or I think I've been a crap mum for not doing something for my kids, my cheeks get a weird sensation and go really hot. Weird AF!

My biggest? Get this... 14 years after splitting up with the kid's dad, I still feel guilty that they don't have an 'intact' mum and dad. My husband still regularly asks me when will I let this finally go?

What's it all about then? Surely there has got to be some scientific explanation for this?

Upon investigation, it seems widely accepted that women experience feelings of guilt approximately 30-40% more than men. The general view is that of women having a more natural lean towards empathy and compassion, meaning we struggle with both habitual (internalised) and interpersonal (how our actions affect others) guilt far easier than men. Whilst most people don't want to hear it these days, there's still an argument to say it's evolutionary in that sense. Elizabeth Shirtcliff, a psychologist and behavioural endocrinologist at the University of New Orleans states "The fact is, men are supposed to feel guilt less intensely because men are, generally, less empathetic than women. It's the way evolution made us. But few people want to talk about it in those terms."

Some argue (a particular Spanish study conducted in 2010) that men need fixing, so they feel guilt more and women needed support, alleviating them from the guilt. I'm not sure this is the answer? We most certainly do not need anymore reasons to make the gender gap any bigger than it already is.

Female guilt feels like a flippin onion - with many, many layers. Whether it's walking past a homeless person, letting a friend down, forgetting to ring your mum, sending the kids on a school trip without their wellies (yes, that is one of my #guiltmemories), feeling like you've got to pick work emails up in the evening when you're supposed to be reading bedtime stories (yeah, that one too), forgetting your BFF's birthday, not helping someone move house, caring for your parents and feeling resentful and finally the classic, feeling guilty for feeling guilty because FFS woman, you've got it far better than a lot of people! Have a fucking word will you! I get it. I've been there. Still go there on occasions. Day trips only, I never take an overnight bag!

Now, here's the stinger that just doesn't compute with me. Evidence shows that women are often the main perpetrators of making other women feel bad. (I'm not totes signed up to the whole of this because I don't believe in the notion that other people MAKE you feel stuff, we CHOOSE what we feel, BUT, and it's a big but, I sadly agree that women can be fucking bitches!) A study from the University of Arizona found that women are often meaner to each other than men are to women. I'm guessing you don't need me to tell you that, right? You've experienced it firsthand? These researchers also found existence of something known as "Queen Bee Syndrome" – the phenomenon of powerful women being disliked disproportionately more by other women than by men (think back to my AFBFH). One reason behind this is because powerful women are seen to violate gender expectations. A good example is former Democratic presidential nominee Hilary Clinton, whose fan base was higher when she was in her supporting role as First Lady, than when she ran for office.

So how do we sort this crock of shit out?? If female guilt is so rife, do we simply suck it up, take it on the chin and learn to live with it? Not on my watch!

It's important to address our individual guilty feelings. It's an emotion so we can use the strategy we learned earlier in getting out of our own way: to question them, to lean into them. To dismantle their power and function. It's time to give a big "Fuck You" to all those people who like to have an opinion on your life. It's time to screw the societal roles so that we can reject the guilt imposed on us by people that do not accept the varied paths that women can, and should, take in their lives. We must ignore those who undermine and belittle, and those who question our lifestyles simply because they are different from their own. It's small-minded bullshit. Oh... and if you're a woman who is brave enough to admit that you have cast guilt onto another woman by being a meany - I applaud your honesty and accountability and DON'T DO IT EVER AGAIN!

I'm quite a practical coach. I like to show people what good looks like. Demonstrate to them that I can walk my talk and give them something to emulate. I like to give people actual things they can DO that work straight away and get them results, so I now feel its a good time to offer up one of my golden nuggets. This is actually one of the most sought-after tools in my toolbox. One of the BIGGEST things women feel guilty about is saying NO to people who ask for help or ask them to do something for them, even if they really want to say No.

I see so many women living life at 100mph, spinning 27,000 plates, multi-tasking with a broom up their arse, flopping onto the sofa at the end of the day looking like they've been dragged through a hedge backwards, feeling like Cinderella. Meanwhile, their partner, kids, colleagues, friends are kicking back and chillaxing.

These women NEVER put themselves first. They put everyone else's needs and priorities above their own. They're tired and weary. They've lost their identity - they look in the mirror and wonder where the youthful, zest-for-life version of themselves has gone. Their self-worth has taken a nose dive and with that, a big chunk of their confidence.

And the worst bit? They're filled to the brim with guilt, resentment and sadness, but they can't see it.

Does that resonate?

Well, it most certainly does not have to be that way!

The good news is that even if you've been in this situation for years, it can be changed. What's important to recognise however, is that it's time to look in the mirror. It's time to stop pointing the finger at other people and blaming them for treating you this way. It's with a good heart that I tell you this... (it might sting a bit) ...

You created this. You allow this to happen. You are an enabler.

OK. I know! You've tried to say NO like a million times though. And they just keep on taking advantage of you! So, what then? You just going to throw the towel in and allow this to continue for the rest of your life? Over my dead body! Persistence beats resistance and a big part of being assertive is having tenacity and grit.

I'm going to make this SUPER EASY for you... see, you like it already!

Learning to say No and to put yourself first needs just a few key ingredients. A little bit of a mindset shift and a smidge of skills development. I'm going to give you a 5-step formula that will have you dishing those No's out like sweeties by the end of the day. It's a practical formula that you can simply plug and play.

When you've finished reading this section, you could walk into the lounge in your home or into a meeting in the office and immediately apply it and get instant results. Is that something that would make positive difference to your life? Good. Let's get cracking then!

There are just five simple steps to get you well on your way to feeling liberated and in control of your own life. Are you ready to take back your power?

1. Have a word with yourself.

This first step is about managing your mindset. Before you even engage your brain to open your mouth, your first words are with yourself. You're likely filled with limiting beliefs around being able to say No. Some of those might be quite deep rooted from your childhood, but that doesn't mean we can't reframe some of those beliefs. Our job here is to get you into a position where you wholeheartedly believe that you have the right to say No and that you grant yourself permission to do so. To help you with this, go back to the Assertive Bill of Rights.

2. Start with a compliment.

So, we've got our mindset in check. We've given ourselves permission to say No.

Let's use a nice, easy (and a bit tongue in cheek) example to demonstrate how this works. So, you're approached in the school playground by one of the PTA mums who asks you if you would take up the position of 'chair' for the next term. This is the last thing on earth you would want to do. This is your third child to go through this school and you've already 'served your time' on the PTA. Using the formula, we start with a compliment which might sound something like this:

" Ah, thanks for asking me Jenny, I'm really flattered that you think I'd be a great chair for the PTA."

It's as simple as that for step 2. Nothing else required.

3. Say No and Own It

Now it's time to deliver your answer. Your job here is to be succinct. It's important that you own it so no trying to give excuses as to why you can't. Remember your rights. You do not have to justify saying No. You can simply not want to. End of. Do your best to refrain from having an episode of waffleitis here (We'll talk more on that in Chapter 6). The temptation will be to carry on talking to fill any awkward silences but I want you to metaphorically hand the uncomfortableness over to them. So, this might sound like something along these lines:

"You know what, I'm not keen on doing another stint on the PTA this year so I'm going to say No, thank you."

That's it. Stop there. Wait for a response.

4. Stay rational, not emotional.

Don't get sucked in. You might likely get a yacky feeling rising in your tummy at this point - that'll be your guilt kicking in. Just notice it, breathe, and it will pass. Keep that dialogue going in your mind that you have the right so say No, this does not make you a bad person. In fact, it makes you a very good person for having your own personal boundaries that allow you to serve yourself and then ultimately be in a position to serve those you love better too. They will get to experience the best version of you.

So, there's nothing to physically say at this point. Just smile.

Remember, you can be assertive and nice at the same time, they are not mutually exclusive.

5. Change the subject and move on.

You might have experienced a tumbleweed moment after you said No, or you may have received an awkward acceptance. Either way, you want to conclude this conversation and move on. The best way to do this is to change the subject. So back to the PTA example.......

"Oh, actually Jenny, glad I bumped into you this morning as I've been meaning to check with you, can Bertie still make it to Rupert's party next Saturday?"

Job. Done.

Now, there is one caveat with this. If you've been a YES person for a very long time, some people are going to be a bit surprised at this new response from you. Therefore, they are likely to start to beg and plead with you to say Yes. This is where it's super important that you dig deep and stick to your guns. The way we do that is to deploy "THE BROKEN RECORD STRATEGY". You simply rinse and repeat. Compliment, Say No and Own It, Change the subject and move on. You might even have to do this three or four times. Remember, persistence beats resistance!

Please don't get cross with people for doing this to you. Remember that look in the mirror? Your old behaviour was breeding that behaviour from them. You've changed your behaviour and so now you will gradually breed a new behaviour in them too. Stick with it!

Right, off you go! Go give it a whirl and report back on your progress. I'd like to hear all about them - successes and car crashes alike - there's learning in them all!

PS.... Please tag me in your #guiltmemories (and use this hashtag obvs). Communal wallowing always helps, right? No, does it shite! But there might be a few shits and giggles in it for us.

Vulnerability

Before you start this section, you might notice a marked difference in my attitude. You see, I've just taken a break (I'm Sunday afternoon writing) and knocked out a lemon meringue pie (I told you in the intro I was mega at those) whilst glugging a bottle of rosé. I have now stepped into my overly confident self, so the rest of this chapter (which I aim to finish tonight) might have a slightly different air about it (although I do have this limiting or maybe unlimiting belief that I produce far higher quality work when I've had a few drinkypoos... does that happen to anyone else too? I'm cock sure it does!)

Anyway, on with vulnerability....

You might be wondering what the feck vulnerability has to do with power?

I thought the same when I first checked in with this stuff. You see, I was one of those stoic, warrior women... what? You too? I classed myself as a super strong woman, tough as old boots, handles anything life throws at her and then some. There were people I knew that I thought should really pull themselves together, get a grip, stop being a big girl's blouse and acting like some kind of pussy. See, there's a whole load of sexist bullshit right there in how I'd been brought up that I never did see in my prime years (who am I kidding, my prime is just beginning! Rah!). But fundamentally, I viewed vulnerability as a weakness.

Big girls' blouse? Why does that make you weak?

A pussy? Last time I checked; pussies were hard AF! Mine has birthed a couple of whoppers and put up with a right number of violations over the years, yet she still bounces back! She's the epitome of resilience (more on that topic later). Balls, on the other hand, shrink at the first sign of a splash of cold water and attempt to climb back up inside their owner and hide... we really must change this perception... add it to the list, will you?

Anyway, I digress (I might do that a bit in the rest of this chapter, please forgive me). Back to vulnerability.

One of my all time heroines is the wonderful Brené Brown. Her book, "Daring Greatly", is one of my fave reads EVER. The opening gambit had me gripped instantly, where she shares that the phrase 'Daring Greatly' is from Theodore Roosevelt's speech "Citizenship in a Republic" and is often referred to as "The man in the arena" (or in this case, we'll go for woman in the arena, yeah?)

Here's the passage that made the speech famous which Brené shares on the first page of her book, but I still want you to go buy it and read it, coz there's like a gazillion golden nuggets in the book that will change you FOREVER!

"It is not the critic who counts; not the man who points out how the strong man stumbles, or where the doer of deeds could have done them better. The credit belongs to the man who is actually in the arena, whose face is marred by dust and sweat and blood; who strives valiantly; who errs, who comes short again and again, because there is no effort without error and shortcoming; but who does actually strive to do the deeds; who knows great enthusiasms, the great devotions; who spends himself in a worthy cause; who at the best knows in the end the triumph of high achievement, and who at the worst, if he fails, at least fails while daring greatly, so that his place shall never be with those cold and timid souls who neither know victory nor defeat."

Brené says this is vulnerability. My fave bit is where she describes it as being "ALL IN", a phrase that has stuck with me ever since and that has become a regular feature in my vocabulary. She goes on to say that "rather than sitting on the sidelines and hurling judgement and advice, we must dare to show up and let ourselves be seen".

So, you see, loads of people have got a wonky perception of what vulnerability means. Brené debunks a load of myths around this, starting with vulnerability being a weakness. It couldn't be further from the truth. Vulnerability sounds like truth and feels like courage, as she puts it. However, what I found enlightening is that when you go too far the other way, that's not vulnerability either. Oversharing. Purging. Indiscriminate disclosure. That's not it. Brené says " Vulnerability is based on mutuality and requires boundaries and trust (both feature in this book). It is about sharing our feelings and experiences with people who have earned the right to hear them. Being vulnerable and open is mutual and an integral part of the trust-building process"

Now that you've heard that do you see how vulnerability fits within our power? When we dare greatly, we put ourselves in the arena. Nobody else can take that away from us. It's not about achieving or failing; it's about allowing yourself to live more fully by getting to know yourself better, revealing your true self and bringing purpose and meaning to your life.

So, what does this mean in terms of how you live your life and the relationship to The Woman Up Way? Well, that's easy. Being vulnerable is a liberating experience. It allows us to step into our own power. It is the gateway to feeling liberated, which is my yardstick measure for everything in life, and allows you to live an authentic life - one that is true to you, with meaning and purpose. For me, that sums up the best life ever.

———

Personal Boundaries

Growing up, I didn't have any personal boundaries. I didn't have a clue what they were. Never even heard of them. I'm determined that this is not the case for my three daughters. I regularly have conversations with them about setting personal boundaries. Why? Because they set you up for success to live in personal power. They also set other people around you up for success as they clearly articulate how they can and cannot behave towards you.

Personal boundaries are guidelines, rules or limits that a person creates to identify reasonable, safe and permissible ways for other people to behave towards them, and how they will respond when someone passes those limits.

When I first encountered this as a concept I was like "Well that all seems a bit rude and obnoxious" - just me? You see, I was brought up to be nice, polite, not make a fuss... and that meant that anything but being agreeable was out of order, really. My mum, my gorgeous, big hearted, amazing mum, had and still has, no personal boundaries and I have witnessed her being taken advantage of on many occasions, and I am ashamed to say, have done it to her myself too. I'd like to think over recent years, I've coached my mum to stand up for herself a bit more and say no to things she doesn't want to do but naturally, she's got some deeply ingrained habitual behaviours that don't serve her and are super hard to shift after all these years. She does, has always and will always, need to be needed by other people. She has no idea what she wants for herself and I think now is too scared to even contemplate the prospect of what that might be. And that makes me really sad. But at the same time, it makes me even more determined to have my own boundaries and help my daughters have theirs.

We can set boundaries for all kinds of things: personal space; sexuality; emotions and feelings; stuff and possessions; time and energy; ethics and principles, to name but a few.

Having boundaries can improve your relationships, boost your confidence and your self-esteem and help you to conserve your emotional energy, which I'm learning at this stage in life is worth it's weight in gold and like rocking horse shit to replenish!

Here are a bunch of classic warning signs that you might lack personal boundaries:

- Your relationships are hard work, difficult and dramatic;
- You find making decisions really hard;
- You really hate letting other people down;
- You have a lot of guilt and anxiety;
- You often feel tired for no apparent reason;
- You overshare when you've only just met someone;
- Shit always happens to you;
- You get really annoyed by people and can be a bit 'off';
- You feel like people don't show you respect;
- You behave passive aggressively e.g., sarcastic, nagging, complaining, silent treatment, huffing and puffing;
- Sometimes you wonder who you really are;
- You are scared of being rejected.

Boundaries aren't hard and fast rules though either. God, if they were, I just wouldn't cope - remember, I'm from the school of "If you obey all the rules, you miss all the fun!" Boundaries are best when flexible and they really shouldn't be things that make you feel unhappy or miserable. So having a boundary of not eating cake would be a really bad one for me! Their job is to protect you, not make your life restricted. They should give you the freedom to be how you want to be by keeping the people around you in check. They should enable joy, not limit it. They are also not about right or wrong. They are based on your values and what's important to you, therefore they might be totally different to someone else's and that's ok. Your personal boundaries are not something for other people to argue with. If other people refuse to accept them then question whether you really want that person in your life anymore. Which brings me onto what to do when boundaries are violated. I know many women who have gone to the effort of setting some boundaries, maybe even communicating them clearly, but then allowed people to completely violate them. There have to be clear consequences for those who overstep the mark. Make sure you build this into your boundary setting exercise!

If someone doesn't like your boundaries, that's their hard cheese! They might have a grumble and a moan but that's their issue, not yours. Send them packing and they'll soon get over it... and learn for next time.

Still not sure what your personal boundaries would be? Do the work then. Start with this bunch of questions and see where it takes you:

- What are the five rules to being my friend? Do I know them quickly and easily?
- What are the 10 things I most like to do with my time? Can I quickly come up with them?
- What are the 10 things I hate doing? Do I even have strong feelings about things?

———

Judgement - Self and Others

I feel in a privileged position that I'm a Gen X girl. Why? Because I got to experience the two sides of life. The one pre social media and the one post. It taught me A LOT.

My biggest fear for my daughters is growing up in a world full of false expectation and being laden with judgement. And not just from other people, but from themselves. It's like our teenage girls have become self-eating monsters. If it's not their appearance - which it is 97% of the time - they're judging each other's thoughts, feelings, decisions, choices. I think if I were a teenager now, I'd lose the plot. I'd feel like I'd lost my marbles. I'm not sure if I could distinguish between what's real and what's not, what I think and what I don't, who I am and who I'm not... OH, and don't forget, who I'm 'supposed' to be! FFS!

I wish judgement would just fuck right off! Here's where we're really screwed up people... we think our judgements are reality, fact. And they're so not. It's just too easy to get attached subconsciously to our opinions. It's all down to those lovely unconscious cognitive biases we've got going on all day long. As humans, we LOVE to think we're right and our biases help us to believe that. One classic is confirmation bias. Our capacity to only see evidence that reinforces what we believe and our brain disregards any evidence to the contrary. You never even get to consciously know it.

Many moons ago, this wasn't too much of an issue but with all this online living it's got a bit out of hand to say the least. Mix that in with people's cowardliness to say what the fuck they like when they're hiding behind a phone screen, that they wouldn't dare say to someone's face and there you have it. Absolute carnage.

Aside from all the hullaballoo it causes (don't even get me started on the number of times I've had to have conversations with the school) what concerns me most is the damage it does to self esteem. Now I know this isn't just a female problem, it's universal. The boys are just as bad. But we've got to get a grip on it somehow. The way to do that? Us Gen X dudes and dudettes have got to role model it to the youth of today. You know that old saying, don't you, behaviour breeds behaviour, well, now is the time to get on that bus!

It's easier said than done (I feel like a broken record the number of times I've said that already in this book), we don't even realise we're doing it. But here's what I want you to consider...

When we judge someone else, it is merely a reflection of ourselves. More simply put, if I judge you for the way you look, that says more about me than it does about you. Make sense? That shines a light on my insecurity. It's likely I'm judging that other person because the green-eyed monster has got the better of me. She had something I don't see in myself. Hmmm, now there's a thought hey?

There's also some wonky neuroscience going on too - you see, we judge others by their behaviour and we judge ourselves by our intent. That's why we always find ourselves having to say "I didn't mean it that way" after we've unwittingly upset someone.

Once you've mastered that (coz that's the easiest part, let me tell you) then you can start to apply the same approach to your judgement of self. During the first lockdown of the Coronavirus pandemic in 2020, my confidence took a massive nose dive. I got myself some therapy pretty sharpish as I could sense where this had the potential to go (plus I'm a firm believer in having therapy 'just because', not just to fix something that is broken. It's like taking your mind to the gym.) Here's what I learned about myself...

For many years, without realising it, due to my corporate career, I had excruciatingly high-performance expectations of myself. When I hit those standards and goals, I chalked them up without so much as a pat on the back and I was onto the next one, never acknowledging my achievements. When I missed them, boy did I give myself a roasting! I would berate myself so badly, in a way that I would never have subjected any other living creature to on this earth! My therapist said I was wicked to myself and described my behaviour as Jekyll & Hyde like.

So, heed this warning... just like there ain't no party like an S Club party, there ain't no judgement like self-judgement. Please... be kind to yourself and be kind to others. You are just one perspective and there are as many perspectives in the world as there are people... oh and btw, none of them are a true version of reality! We're all just bumbling along making our own versions of shit up! Boom... I'll just leave that one there with you.

———

Competition, Collaboration and Compromise

The 3 C's! One of may fave topics. Are we still talking about power? Course we are!

After we've come this far through the chapter, this one is easy peasy to get your noggin round.

If you think back to when I shared with you the ingredients of assertiveness right back a the beginning and we looked at the four quadrants, you may have some distant recollection of my thoughts on compromise. If you missed it, I said it was shit! Enuff said. Go back and read it again if it didn't sink in.

So, remember, we're in the realms of personal power here - what do you think is the preferred approach between competition and collaboration? Yep, you nailed it. Collaboration is THE FUTURE. Especially when it comes to embarking on your journey to Woman Up. Let's leave competition where it belongs, at the Olympics (and obvs the mums/dads' races at Sports Day). I'm kiddin'. There are certainly places for competition, I'm not going to list them all here but generally speaking, restrict it to competing in sport. I actually can't think of any others. You might be thinking, well, what about in business? Traditionally, yes. Businesses would compete against their competitors. But I don't know if you've woken up and smelt the coffee recently? The most successful organisations are those that are collaborating... yes, some of them EVEN with their competitors. And when it comes to women... well, we're just so much more successful when we work together. The reality of the sitch however is that women can be catty, back stabbing, bitches. Generally speaking (oh god, I'm opening myself up for a trolling here, but sod it!) at least when men compete, they're open about it. They run onto the metaphorical pitch waving their dicks about like swords at dawn. Everyone knows what's going on. And when the match is over, it's over. They all get naked and have a bubble bath together (that's just weird). But with women, it's an underhand affair. It's sneaky and shady and all so terribly two-faced... Oh, and the grudge goes on for, like, EVER.

I hope I've made my point here in a power context. Life is most certainly sweeter and more pleasant when we work together. Collaboration, as Stephen Covey put it, is when the whole is greater than the sum of the parts. I genuinely and wholeheartedly believe that when women come together, build each other up and empower each other, great things happen! What it takes is a mindset of abundance - there is enough to go around for everybody - instead of operating from a scarcity mindset - there is only so much and I must fight for it.

So, my big ask is this... Go out there and link arms with other women. Make good shit happen together. Pool your talents and resources. Jim Rohn, a motivational speaker, said

 "You are the average of the 5 people you spend most time with."

I urge you to choose those five carefully. Cut the toxic people from your life and replace them with wholesome, supportive, collaborative people, who are positive and possess an abundance mentality! Empowered women, empower women. That's why Ladies Life Lounge, my online members club for

women that I run with Roxy, is so flippin brilliant. We have a team of ten Resident Experts who run their own businesses but support our club with their expertise. It's a total win-win because we get the expertise we need and they get access to our juicy big audience! (Mic drop.)

Before I finish this section, an important note on the trolling thing. I strongly recommend you do not troll me. Why? (Well, aside from it simply being absolute vile behaviour) Not because I'm a righteous cow but because you play straight into my hands. I say this with zero sarcasm too. If you troll me, you are a classic demonstration of passive aggressive, which I've already pointed out is the lowest of the low. I will naturally respond in a very assertive manner meaning you are left looking perfectly like one of my ideal clients. I will therefore attempt to get you to come on one of my programmes and I will change your life forever! (Maybe I've just shot myself in the foot and sold it to you, idk.)

———

It's None of Your Business What Other People Think of You - How Not to Give a Fuck About What Other People Think

Look, this is something that people have life-long battles with. (Not gonna lie, me included.) I'm not going to attempt to cure you of this in one book. But hell, get from up your own arse, will you! Here's something I learned from one of my first business coaches, the renowned, Lisa Johnson - "The truth of the matter is, it's none of your business what other people think of you". (Link up with Lisa at @lisajohnsonstrategist) Don't flatter yourself that they're even bothered, or they've given you the slightest thought.

The irony is that everyone's so caught up in their own head, wondering what everyone is thinking of them, that nobody has got time to be thinking stuff about other people. You follow me?

That's the easiest way to let go of giving a fuck about what other people think of you. My biz bestie, Rox, is an absolute GENIUS on this topic. Head to my FREE resources page to watch her Womanifest™ talk on the subject to learn more - it's EPIC! (Warning: make sure you have tissues. You WILL cry!)

The other way is to learn to validate yourself internally. If I asked you the question 'Do you look to others for feedback on how you did, or do you look to yourself to assess your performance?' What would your answer be?

Most people who give too much of a fuck what other people think of them are external validators. I most certainly was, and still am to an extent. However, I've learnt over time how to be my own coach, judge and jury, and to be happy with my own assessments of how I did in a given situation. How did I do that? Practice. Pressing my pause button when I felt tempted to seek external validation, then sitting with myself and my thoughts and reflecting (I've never been much of a natural reflector, always the activist me). Eventually, I began to draw my own conclusions and built evidence around me to endorse them. Bingo. Give it a whirl. What have you got to lose? A whole lotta brain fart, that's what.

Ok, so here we are at the end of the Chapter on Power. Is it what you thought it would be? I'm guessing not so much. The picture should be starting to come together now. A bit less blurry. Your mindset will be starting to shift, millimetre by millimetre. We're at the halfway mark now. Take this opportunity to have a breather. I know I'm going to. I'm just about to go and make a cuppa, cut myself a nice slice of that lemon meringue and sit down for the grand finale episode of Line of Duty season 7 - who is H?

If, when you're reading this, you've never watched Line of Duty, you really are missing out on life! I urge you to put this book down and go binge watch all 7 seasons! I'll still be here waiting for you when you get back... but don't forget about me, will you? x

SIX

COMMUNICATION

You Can't NOT Communicate

COMMUNICATION IS SUCH A BROAD TOPIC. It drives me bonkers when I see examples of PDP's (Personal Development Plans to those of you who were lucky enough to escape this process!) that tell people to improve their communication skills - WTF? There's never been a stronger example of a goal that is set up to fail. We talk about communication skills but it's just an umbrella term. Beneath it is a vast sub-set of skills. Let's just take the basic ones for now, like listening and questioning. The point I want to make at the outset of this chapter is that you can't NOT communicate.

Lots of people think that by saying nothing, they're not communicating however, saying nothing sometimes says EVERYTHING, right? You know how it is. So, when it comes down to the crunch of whether you are going to successfully Woman Up or not, a whole heap of your success is riding on your ability to communicate well. That's gonna mean learning some new and specific skills and then practising them till you're shit hot at them. I often get asked why I'm so good at being assertive or articulating something clearly and succinctly. I wasn't born that way. I've spent the last 10 years honing my craft. They say it takes around 10,000 hours to become a master in your chosen craft, so you gotta put the graft in.

So, I'm keen to start this chapter with the absolute basics. Please don't take offence at this. I'm not trying to teach a granny to suck eggs (another really weird saying). The reason I want to go there is because what I notice most in this era of tech and complexity is that we've lost the art of doing the basics well. We have a classic knowing - doing gap. We know exactly what to do and can describe how to do it but in practice, we just don't - we think we do, but that's just really low self-awareness.

Off for a trip down memory lane to Mehrabian's Rule. You'll know this when you see it.

Albert Mehrabian defined the elements of communication really simply, using the following approach:

So, you don't need to be a rocket scientist to see that over half of our ability to communicate lies in our body language (that would include things like eye contact and facial expressions too), and a fair old whack of what's left is down to tone. Now in this day and age (sound like a right old fart now, don't I?), we've lost the art of this because we don't use the two biggest resources that we have available to ourselves. The majority of the planet now heavily depend on just 7% of their ability to land a message the way they intended. That sounds crackers to me when you say it out loud - just why would you do that? It makes no sense? No flippin wonder the world has gone to shit! Nobody understands anyone else. When we send emails and text messages all day long it's no wonder things get misconstrued and taken the wrong way, because they never stood a flippin chance in the first place.

The added challenge is that the women of the world have this unique ability to read all kinds into things! We love to guess, speculate, assume and jump to conclusions. We love a bit of drama and before we know it, things have blown right out of proportion.

If only we could just at least pick up the phone instead of sending a text. If only we could just get off our arses and walk across the office for a face to face conversation rather than pinging that email... the world would be a better and easier place that lived in a damn sight more harmony. Just that. It'll blow your socks off just how powerful it is in you being perceived the way you intended, showing that you actually care or that something is important to you. Your credibility will sky rocket, whether that's in work, business or your personal life. I know you want that deep down. I also know that you're scared. Go back to vulnerability and step up for yourself. You deserve it.

———

There's Nowt as Queer as Folk

Proper right northern saying this in't it? I love it! But it's true. There's nowt as queer as folk. The world would be such a boring place if we were all the same but we don't half get ourselves in a tizz when we find someone a bit different to get along with.

You may have heard the phrase 'people like people like themselves'. We're naturally drawn to people who have a sense of sameness, after all, at a primal level we all crave a strong sense of belonging, to have found our 'tribe', so to speak.

But listen up, if you really want to make your own way in this world and live life to the full, living your best life, it's going to require you to be like a chameleon (or at least learn a minimum of three additional languages). What? Chill your beanz, let me explain. The success all lies in your ability to adapt and be flexible (think communication yoga) and to be able to tweak your language in a way that plays to the other person - like music to their ears, you get me?

Sometimes, when people don't 'get us' or misunderstand what we mean, we point the finger at them for not getting it. That's totes topsy turvy. If someone doesn't understand you, then that's on you. You did a shit job of landing it. It's time to look in the mirror.

A really simple way to look at this is that we each have a behavioural preference, a way of communicating that is linked to our values, motivations, learning style etc. You may have done one of those psychometric tests at some point in your career like Myers Briggs, DISC (Dominance; Influence; Steadiness; Conscientiousness), Insights or SDI (Strength Deployment Inventory). Basically, what they show us is that we each speak a different language, or more typically and broadly speaking we tend to fall into one of four categories. SDI has always been my fave as it helps you to explore yourself and others, both when things are going well and when they are going not so well. It also doesn't put you in a box. You get a unique position on a triangle (that has thousands of available positions) and so it gives you a real sense of how you do things. (If you want one of those doing, give me a shout) Now, back to my knowing - doing gap theory. Loads of people have done one of these and they all know their preference, but do they use it every day? Do they bollocks! It's not good being a learning junkie and never taking any action with what you've learned.

You don't even need to do one of these assessments to tap into this. We don't all walk round handing out questionnaires to people we meet and ask them to fill it in before we'll engage in a conversation with them - that would be weird! Instead, we read the clues in people's behaviour and look for congruence that leads us to have a reasonable sense of how they prefer to communicate. I've often been called a bit of a witch for being able to figure people out within 60 seconds of meeting them. It freaks people out! I'll tell you a little story about that...

I was once working on a project for a large utilities business where all of their engineers from all over the country were taken through a service transformation programme. There were thousands of them and so we held events at footballs stadiums all around the country, with 250 of them attending at a time. During the day we would take them into breakout groups of approximately 15 people, and do a whistle stop lesson on behavioural preferences. It was a very male dominated environment as you can imagine, and I was often challenged hard by these guys, especially being a woman training them - some of them didn't like that. Anyway, I welcomed my group into the room and this guy, Tony, at the back, sat there slouched with his legs wide open like some wide boy, says "Who are you and what do you do?" I politely introduced myself and moved on. Now we had this cool little trick that we used to do. We would hand out the questionnaires for them to complete and a pencil with which to complete it. We had 4 different colours of pencils that each represented one of the preferences. Our task was to secretly hand out the pencils by giving the colour to the person that we figured matched their preference, judging by the way they have behaved in the first 5 minutes of the session. I gave Tony a red pencil. Once they had completed the task, I asked the group by way of a show of hands, who had come out as a red preference. Tony raised his hand. I responded with "Ooh, that's funny Tony, look, you've got a red pencil. You know you asked me what I do at the beginning of the session? Well, I'm a pencil scientist". He was so freaked out, he threw the pencil out of his hand on to the floor and shouted "No way, fuck off. You're some kind of witch". The rest of the lads we're howling with laughter and I earned my credibility stripes with the group, including Tony, at that moment. I'd adapted my style to suit my audience.

I have also fucked it up beautifully! It was early in my Exec Coaching days, I'd not long qualified and I got the opportunity to coach a Chief Finance Officer of a big, well-known company. I was pooing my pants!!! Anyway, he had relationship issues with his CEO that we were trying to work through. When we talked, he never used to look at me, he would always look down and draw geometric shapes on a piece of paper, like Tetris. I thought this was a bit rude, tbh! But then, I'm a yellow (extroverted, creative, big picture). I'm sure you can imagine, as the CFO, he was NOT remotely yellow; he was outright blue (introverted, data driven, detailed). We couldn't have been more different (and therefore speaking different languages). I made the biggest booboo by asking him how he felt about something. He slammed his pen down on the table, looked up at me and said "I don't FEEL anything". You can imagine how much I blushed! But it was a mega lightbulb moment for me. I'd simply got one word wrong. Instead of 'how does that make you FEEL?' It just needed to be 'what do you THINK about that?' DOH! #anotherschoolgirlerror

So, the moral of the story is this... Embrace the fact that we are all different, value that diversity. The best teams, groups of friends, families have people that have a blend of preferences. Go out of your way to adapt to others; it actually gets you the results you want, so it's worth it!

Whether it's your partner at home, your kids, friends or family members, peers at work, stakeholders, boss, whoever... this is the magic sauce!

I started this section with a very northern saying and I want to end on a point about accents and dialect in the way we communicate. I meet many women who are ashamed of their accent and try to cover it up. I totes get this because I once had a manager who was a complete buffoon to say the least, had zero credibility with me, in fact, I had no respect for her either.

She observed and assessed me delivering a leadership training event one day and gave me some feedback at the end. She told me that I needed elocution lessons because my mancunian/scouse cross accent wasn't professional. It scarred me for quite some time. That was until, one evening after several hotel bar vinos with two of my well-respected coaching colleagues, they helped me to finally challenge it. What turned out to actually be true was that people loved me FOR my accent. It made me approachable, 'normal' and down to earth. The following day we were running an assessment centre for a client, and we were doing the wash up. I spoke out with some observations that challenged another assessor's perception of a candidate and I didn't try to dress it up, I just said it how I wanted to. Rick (one of my coaching colleagues) was sat behind me and handed me this little note in the image below. In case you can't read it, it says *"This is you at your brilliant, northern best"*. Since then, I've been able to proudly let my northerness shine as the true authentic me I was always intended to be. And this little piece of paper has remained on my office wall as a daily reminder.

It's easy to get caught up in the elements of communication that aren't really important but can hold us back. The task is to get past that and into the real skill elements that I've talked about in this section, so if you've had a similar experience to me, then it's time to let your authentic, brilliant self out, whatever your accent, and get focused on learning to speak the different communication languages!

———

The Power of Language

OK, so I know I said earlier that only 7% of the way we communicate is down to words, but that doesn't mean they don't matter. Words are powerful. Like really fucking powerful.

You know I'm partial to the odd saying or two... well here's another fave of mine:

 "It's not what you say, it' how you say it".

You've come across that one before, right? 100% True dat.

More often than not, communication goes tits up because our intent didn't match our impact. You'll know if this has ever happened to you if you've found yourself saying "well, I didn't mean it like that".

The same message can sound so different with a different choice of words. I want to take you right back to one of the three mindsets we covered at the start of this book - accountability. Now I know we set accountability up as a mindset, and that's correct, but we 'demonstrate' that mindset to other people in the way we act and behave. Specifically, we can tell how accountable someone is by the language they use. Let's run through a couple of examples:

"Unfortunately, there's not much I can do about that. You'll have to speak to the other department."

Can you tell I get really pissed off when I get a response like this when I ring somewhere up? It's a classic and a really simple example to show the effects. What's wrong with that phrase? Do you find it uplifting or draining? Which words in that phrase are having a negative impact on you?

You'll likely pull out: unfortunately; not much; have to.

This statement can be easily transformed into something like this:

"I can absolutely help you with that. We have a team of experts who specifically handle this type of query every day, I'll get you through to them right now."

See the difference? It's much more positive, it's focused on what can be done, not what can't. It has more energy about it, it 'feels' good and it's accountable! Yet, I've said EXACTLY the same thing.

Let's do another. A more personal example:

"You make me feel like shit coz you do fuck all to help around this house."

How about:

"Let's split the chores in the house this weekend so we box them off quickly and we can get out for some quality time together."

You're far more likely to get some support off the latter statement than the former. Go on, give it a whirl and see what happens. If you need a bit of help, come and find me on socials and tag me in for a transformation phrase.

Here's a bunch of words I'd recommend you delete from your vocabulary because they are really naff:

- Unfortunately.
- Possibly.
- It might be....
- It could be....
- It should be ok....
- I think.
- I can't.
- I/You'll have to.
- I/You must.
- I/You need to.
- I/You've got to.
- There's not much I can do.

Notice how a lot of these words lack certainty. They are wishy-washy. They don't give people confidence in what you're saying and therefore you lack conviction and influence. They're very limiting and a bit 'meh'.

Here's some suggestions of replacements to get you out the starting blocks:

- There's a good chance that....
- What I can do is...
- The best option is....
- It's important that....
- I recommend you....
- My best advice is....

A brief word on swearing. I fucking love swearing! And apparently, I read an article a while back that said that people who swear are way more intelligent. I'll take that. I find it a wonderful stress reliever and a helpful way to articulate when I'm hugely passionate about something. Swearing in context works. Swearing at somebody is outright rude and aggressive. The End.

———

How to Have Influence and Get Yourself Heard in a World Full of Noise

It's really flippin hard to get yourself heard sometimes, isn't it?

Maybe you've had an experience like the ones I have on numerous occasions? See if this one resonates with you...

I was in a leadership role heading up a Learning & Development team for a big company. Every month I would go to the management meeting where I would share my insights and recommendations to improve service, drive up sales, shift the culture etc. And it almost always fell on deaf ears. Next minute, the head honcho would have brought in a bunch of consultants that cost a gazillion quid who would fanny about doing "deep dives" around the business, only to feedback what I had been saying for months! It was infuriating! I just couldn't believe how invisible I was. It really battered my confidence and self-worth too.

Only when I stepped across the consulting threshold and became one of those people that were brought in, did I really begin to get it. All of a sudden, I was listened to. My recommendations were implemented. Now sadly, in those early stages, the only difference was that I was external and they could clearly see the cold hard cash that was being spent and they wanted a good return on that. It was too easy, when I was the internal woman, to just see me as part of the furniture and not acknowledge that I was a cost to this business too. I allowed this to be an excuse for some time. That was until I was really put through my paces by an extremely demanding client, and I had to up my game, pronto. He was a hard-faced bastard - bit of a slave driver too, very righteous with quite shitty intent. He was always trying to trip you up. Now, I had options. I could either play him at his own game or I could take the higher ground. You know what I chose, right?

I spent a significant amount of time learning about influence. If you've never read Robert Cialdini's book, "Influence: The psychology of persuasion", then I highly recommend you do. It gave me a sound foundation and opened my eyes up to explore further.

Here's what I learned relatively quickly...

1. People don't know what it means to influence. We're back to those wonky perceptions. It is not the same as persuasion, negotiation or manipulation, although people get their wires crossed with these. Know the difference and recognise that influence is a higher alternative. A preferred approach that will get you a higher yield and keep your credibility in tact.
2. There are thousands of ways you can influence - different approaches, techniques, models, methods. For me, it is underpinned by some key premises and certain qualities that allow you to influence at a high level. Make it your mission to create a toolkit. Don't be a one trick pony.
3. Be ready to go the distance and top up your tenacity tanks. It takes a huge amount of energy and perseverance when you are influencing well. It's super important that you're uber present and that you're actually listening twice as much as you're talking (God

gave you two ears and one mouth for a reason). Be prepared and ok with having your mind changed.

Long story short, I won this guy over. I demonstrated to him that I had his best interests at heart and my mission was to deliver the results he needed - we wanted the same thing. To achieve that, it was important that he respected me for my expertise but it was my job to demonstrate to him that I knew my shit before he would let his guard down and trust me.

If you want to get heard in a world full of noise, it's time to add influencing to your development plan. It is a skill. It can be learned. I've got tonnes of influencing goodies in my FREE Woman Up Way resources section here: bit.ly/woman-up-FREE-resources. There's a questionnaire, Top 10 Hacks and even a toolkit you can download - knock yourself out on me!

———

Do You Suffer From Waffleitis?

There was this woman I used to work with a number of years ago. She was a gregarious, bubbly lady. Large as life, heart of gold, mad as a box of frogs. She would do anything for anyone, most supportive people leader in the business at that time but boy, when it came to communicating with her, it was painful. Why? Because she would say 27 million words when 6 would do. During a conversation my head would metaphorically roll off the back of my shoulders (Do you remember the 1990 Reach Toothbrush classic "Flip Top Head" TV Commercial – that's the image that springs to mind... YouTube it!)

My point here is this: many women I work with, and even interact with or observe on a daily basis, suffer from a condition I call 'waffleitis'. The inability to be succinct, specific, to the point. Waffleitis is a condition that causes you to 'go round the houses', so to speak - fill the awkward silences with blether, use lots of filler words or fancy language and repeat yourself over again. Is that you?

I LOVE helping women to move from Waffleitis to Well Said. The reason? Because it makes such a positive difference to women's sense of self-worth, confidence and capability (not to mention pay packet!). Waffling does nothing for your credibility or influence. It basically crushes it. People switch off. They zone out. They don't hear (let alone listen) to what you're saying. They get bored. They don't see how what you're saying benefits them. The result? No voice at the table, zero influence on decisions, lack of opportunity to progress, lower performance appraisal and bonus. Even in a personal sense at home and with friends, these same challenges apply – kids don't do what you ask them to do, partner never listens to you, friends talk over you.

I'm guessing I've resonated with many women out there on this one. This is the low-grade crap that you've been tolerating for years as it's been grinding away at you slowly. A few sighs here, feeling a bit deflated there, resentment for others who are getting it right, tears in the car on the way home, flopping onto the sofa in the evening with a bottle of wine to drown it out...

Ok, so enough of that. It's time to take action and I am here to help you do it. There is so much you can do to change this situation but for the purposes of this book, I'm going to focus on just 5 practical tips that will guarantee you get heard and land your message with impact.

1. Let's go old school. There's no point in reinventing the wheel here. In this technological age, we've lost the art of human communication. I want you to think back to Mehrabian's communication theory – the pie chart on Words (7%), Tone (38%) and Body Language (55%). This theory is all about how we communicate meaning with our message, the feelings and attitudes around things i.e., like or dislike. It's important to have congruence through these three elements in your message and do your best to take advantage of all of them. I see many people who say a lot of words but have nothing in terms of the paralinguistics (the way that it's delivered) or the facial expression. For example, if you're excited about something, show it. You've seen the guy right who says "I'm really excited" with no energy, monotone

voice and a face like a wet weekend, right? Don't be that guy/gal!

2. Practice 6-word stories. This helps you to be more succinct. So, tell the story of Cinderella in just 6 words. My example – glass, slipper, ball, get's, her, man. Try it with other well known stories to get you in the groove of it, then turn it to your work/business messages. If you're going into a meeting and you have a slot on the agenda, write down the message you want to land in just 6 words beforehand. Then, build it into 12 words, after that maybe 18. Do you best to stick as closely as you can to this and when you've said it. Zip it (or end it with a question).

3. We've spoken about this earlier so go dig out those dusty old personality/behavioural profiling test results you've got. Whether it's Myers Briggs, Insights, SDI etc., it really doesn't matter. You won't be heard or have influence if you're harping on about employee engagement to the CFO when you're the H.R. Business Partner. Quite frankly, he or she is unlikely to give a monkey's whether everyone is feeling good in their work. You've got to talk to that person in their currency... which is likely to be cold, hard, cash, or at least some bottom line, tangible result. And it is still absolutely possible to land your message about the importance of employee engagement, you just need to do your homework to be able to clearly demonstrate the tangible impact it has on the business.

4. Slow down. A simple one but highly effective. Waffleitis makes us speed up in speech which, combined with lots of words, is what results in verbal

diarrhoea. Not a great strategy. So, very deliberately, slow your speech down and remember to powerfully pause when you land a particular pertinent message (a bit uncomfortable I know at first, but practice makes peachy. I use a little visualisation strategy for this. I imagine the uncomfortableness as a ball in my hands and I picture myself handing that ball to the other person in that moment.)

5. Last but not least – start with the end in mind. If you want to have someone, or a room of people hanging off your every word, then you've got to grab their attention from the word GO! I suggest starting with a 'disturb' – a fact, a statistic perhaps that is slightly alarming or really appealing. For example, if I'm meeting with the CFO again, and I'm presenting my budget request proposal, I might start with '£3.2 million – that's the figure my proposal will deliver back to the business this financial year. Would you like to hear how?' I don't just sit down and commence death by PowerPoint by talking through my proposal page by page.

These 5 tips should get you well on your way to landing your message with impact. And there is SO MUCH MORE! Let's not run before we can walk... Get going with these first and you'll see a marked improvement in the responses you get.

———

Behaviour Breeds Behaviour - Look in the Mirror v's Pointing the Finger

I want to draw this chapter on communication to a close by bringing home a really important message that I've touched on, but not landed explicitly.

Behaviour breeds behaviour

If you do not like the way someone is behaving towards you, change the way you behave towards them - honestly, you'll be blown away by the difference that it makes.

Take a long, hard look in the mirror and ask yourself this question...

What is it that I'm doing or not doing that is helping or hindering this situation?

Look to identify ways that you can modify your own behaviour in order to positively impact the other person. Here's a classic example that happened for me.

When my eldest daughter first became a teenager, I was riddled with fear about letting her have some independence and go out alone, in case she did the things that I used to do when I was her age. However, suffocating her like that only drives her to keep secrets and tell lies so she can do the things that she wants to do. Result? I end up with the outcome that I most feared.

I gave this some thought and decided to change my approach. I told my daughter that the answer would always be yes, as long as she was honest and truthful with me about her plans. I agreed with her that she would only ever get in trouble for lying, never for getting in a precarious situation. She could always call me and I would positively respond. That changed everything. She now talks to me so much more about her life and I know far more than I ever would have done. It means we have a great relationship and she has much safer experiences in which to explore her own identity and independence.

So, whether that be a similar scenario for you, or it's your partner, your parents, your boss, your team, it really doesn't matter. If you want to see a change in someone else's behaviour, first change yours.

SEVEN
EMOTION

Conflict, Confrontation and Challenge

HERE'S a regular thing I hear from women – they're told they're way too emotional in the workplace. Funny that, because I've never known a man get that kind of feedback. I want to ask you a question actually, before we get into the detail: what emotions spring to mind when you think of the woman and then the man. I'll bet it was getting upset or crying for the woman and being too aggressive for the man... am I right? There's one issue right there.

Let's start with the obvious stuff here for a minute. Humans are emotional creatures. We're designed that way. It's a good thing. It should be celebrated! I'm a huge advocate for bringing emotion back to the workplace – things have gone too far... I walk into corporate offices these days and see zombies, clones of each other. Clinical, dead spaces with no vibe or atmosphere. No fire in anyone's belly. Everyone is too wrapped up in their own introverted energy, not wanting to be seen as the one that's a bit different. There's a desire to conform, to blend in. It's grey, it's boring and it has no soul! It's 'wrong' to have any emotion or even half a personality! Who wants to work in a culture like that?

So, for clarity, when I talk about emotions, I want you to recognise that it's not exclusive or limited to the ones mentioned above, nor in that context. Think about the vast array of emotions that can be experienced and demonstrated by all genders and people, however they choose to identify. From anger, frustration and confusion to excitement, elation, nervousness or shame, humiliation and embarrassment.

Let's start with the good news. Generally speaking, women are a little more emotionally intelligent than men. This means you can see this as an opportunity rather than a limitation or a threat. So, let's begin with shifting that mindset. As women, we're more intuitive. We 'sense' things more. We're naturally more present and notice things, especially the unsaid. And there's a big gaping hole in business and society crying out for someone to step in and hold that space. So, let's take it. Trust your natural instincts and capabilities and own it. Use it as your competitive advantage. I'll guarantee if you're able to shift your mindset in this way you will naturally start to behave differently and you'll get immediate results.

Many people, not just women, do struggle when it comes to handling conflict, confrontation and challenge. It tends to trigger people's fight or flight response because they 'see' it as a threat. Similarly, to my point above, progress starts with a mindset shift. That shift is learning to see an opportunity rather than a threat. To do that means becoming more curious. To get out of your own head and into theirs.

Ask yourself the question:

"What's going on for them right now and how can I best serve them in order to serve myself?"

It's metaphorically moving from the 'facing each other across a table' position to 'standing by their side and walking along beside them' position. When you're able to do this, you'll avoid your own amygdala hijack (I'll explain that in a mo).

In handling confrontation, conflict and challenge, there are some really practical approaches and techniques that you can use in order to come out the other side with your credibility firmly intact:

The biggest tip I will offer you is to completely avoid using the phrase "I disagree". Why? Because it's like adding fuel to the flames and you know it. Because you'll likely have had your fingers burnt before (or you've at least witnessed it). Instead, with your curiosity still engaged, listen first. Listen, purely to understand, not to prepare your next response or anticipating the moment they draw breath that gives you a gap in airtime to jump in. Clarify that you understand them fully. Then offer to share an alternative viewpoint. It might sound something like this:

"OK, it's useful to hear the situation from your perspective, can I just check I've completely understood you (then clarify). I can see where you're coming from. I have a bit of a different view that's important is considered, can I share that with you?"

That's the assertive response. It leads with consideration and listening, but follows through with courage. Notice also that it's not focused on the people involved, it's focused on what's important.

You may still get quite a confrontational response to that. When you do, manage yourself carefully. Keep your influence intact. You can do this by ensuring you respond proactively, rather than react in the moment. When we react, we do so based on moods, feelings and circumstance – a recipe for disaster. When we press the pause button and respond, we're able to do so based on principles and desired results.

In this example, my recommendation is that you move to a position of personal boundaries with a little bit of feedback. State your intent first (and make sure that intent is clean and good) e.g. "I want this project to be a success just as much as you do".

Follow that with specifics about the behaviour that you find unacceptable and the impact it has... "shouting at me in that way is not ok. I find it intimidating and that isn't going to help me be my best. It's unacceptable. Please stop it."

Then zip it. Even if that means a bit of a tumbleweed moment. Don't get sucked into filling the black whole of silence with waffle. Let it hang, it's doing it's job. It's powerful. Hold the space for the other person to respond. Just continue to care, and let that show on your face.

That should do the trick and you'll likely get a shift at that moment, maybe even an apology. But if not... its time to take control and end the conversation for some cooling off time.

Feel within your rights to say "I don't wish to continue this conversation and be spoken to in this way. I think it best we take a break and reflect."

What's important here is that you do follow up. Don't leave the ball in their court. Go back, call or send a message later that day or the following day to discuss it.

Conflict, confrontation and challenge don't need to be scary subjects. If we shift our mindset to see them as an opportunity rather than a threat, as well as invest in our skill level and capability/competence at handling them, things should turn out rather peachy!

———

The Competitive Advantage - Emotional Intelligence

So, I mentioned that women tend to be a little more emotionally intelligent than men. Some research would argue that, but I have enough experiences under my belt of interacting with all kinds of people to have made this conclusion for myself.

I really do see this as a competitive advantage! Why, when women are so often criticised for being emotional? Let's start with getting super clear on what emotional intelligence is all about as it's become a bit of a leadership buzzword over the years and I'm keen to make it more relevant to the everyday and our personal, as well as our professional, relationships.

Emotional intelligence is the ability to understand, use, and manage your own emotions in positive ways to relieve stress, communicate effectively, have empathy with others, overcome challenges and defuse conflict. Emotional intelligence helps you build stronger relationships, be successful, and achieve your career and personal goals. It can also help you to connect with your feelings, turn intention into action, and make informed decisions about what matters most to you.

It's defined by four attributes:

1. Self-management – Being able to control impulsive feelings and behaviours, manage your emotions in healthy ways, take initiative, follow through on commitments, and adapt to changing circumstances.
2. Self-awareness – Being able to recognise your own emotions and how they affect your thoughts and

behaviour. You know your strengths and weaknesses, and have self-confidence.

3. Social awareness – You have empathy. You can understand the emotions, needs, and concerns of other people, pick up on emotional cues, feel comfortable socially.

4. Relationship management – You know how to develop and maintain good relationships, communicate clearly, inspire and influence others, work well in a team, and manage conflict.

It's not always the 'clever people' that get on in life. In fact, when it comes to the real 'grown up stuff', they rarely do. You probably know people who smashed it out of the park at school and yet are socially inept. IQ isn't enough on its own to achieve success in life. Yes, your IQ can help you get into Uni, but it's your EQ that will help you manage the stress, emotions, and all the bullshit that will require you to have some 'life skills' that schools just don't equip young people with (don't let me get on my soap box about that!).

Emotional intelligence is vital to help you perform in your job, to your physical and mental health, to your relationships and to your social intelligence (without it, you can end up stressed. Uncontrolled stress raises blood pressure, suppresses the immune system, increases the risk of heart attacks and strokes, contributes to infertility, and speeds up the ageing process. It can also make you more vulnerable to anxiety and depression).

You can grow your emotional intelligence by working on developing those four areas and I believe it's far easier for women to do than men. We have a natural tendency towards it. It's more intuitive to women. I reckon it's a primal thing. We're built to connect on an emotional level.

Here's the watchout though, the bit that might have gotten you in trouble. If you haven't really had the self-awareness around your emotions over the years and you struggle to self-manage, then you'll likely have got some of that feedback at some point that you're too emotional. This skill, and the four attributes, can take years to hone, but here's a really quick win to get you some positive results immediately...

Start by noticing what triggers cause an emotional flare up for you - what is the emotion, where does it manifest itself in your body and what does it feel like?

For example, when I get angry, I feel it in my chest and it feels quite jittery and flappy and my heart beats really fast. When I'm embarrassed or ashamed I feel it in my tummy and it's like a washing machine and I feel a bit nauseous.

Once you can do that bit, your job is to then describe your emotion rather than display it. It makes a world of a difference! Instead of going batshit crazy because you're absolutely fuming, you can calmly articulate it by saying something like "I'm really angry right now because you've let me down by missing the deadline". So, you see, you don't have to bury your emotions or leave them at the door, but what is important is that you can describe them rather than display them. And sometimes, it absolutely warrants a display of emotion (especially when they're positive ones), the important point is that you proactively choose when you display and when you describe, based on the outcomes you are trying to achieve.

Sometimes our emotional displays can end up detracting from the point and other times they can absolutely nail it for us!

———

The Amygdala Hijack - What Happens in the Brain

I mentioned towards the beginning of this chapter that I'd explain the amygdala hijack. Here goes...

Seriously, understanding this was an absolute game-changer for me! It didn't mean that I necessarily 'did' anything differently, but purely 'getting myself' and knowing what was happening, chemically, inside my body really settled me and gave me a strong sense of grounding, alleviating any panic I felt in the moment.

OK, so, you may have come across the fight or flight response before? When we are faced with what we perceive as a threat, we revert to either of these responses, actually, there's three - fight, flight or freeze. We either put up a fight, run off or become paralysed - a bit like a rabbit in headlights. Now in modern day times, the threats that we face are not those that our bodies were designed for. We were designed for escaping from real, physical danger, so we did need to run, fight or try and keep still and hide. The threats we face these days are less physical and more psychological e.g., conflict, confrontation and challenge. However, we still have the same primal response.

The part of our brain responsible for all of this is our amygdala - two small parts at the base of the brain, one in each hemisphere. It is part of our limbic system. Its job is to create emotional memories - draw meaning from emotions and associate them with situations and responses.

Now ordinarily, our frontal lobes would respond to mild threat and they have the ability to do this rationally and logically. However, when the threat feels significant or super strong, the amygdala overtakes the frontal lobes and causes more irrational behaviour and over reaction to situations.

This is because your body is very quickly flooded with the stress hormones, cortisol and adrenaline. Why? To relax your airways, opening them up so you can take in more oxygen, increase the blood flow to your muscles for maximum speed and strength, increase your blood sugar for more energy and dilate your pupils to enhance your vision. In doing so, very little blood flow is supporting those frontal lobes and so your ability to rationalise and make decisions when you need it most goes out the flippin window!

Ahh! That makes sense, right? Now you get it too!

When I experience this now, I'm able to simply talk myself through what is happening and it helps me to keep those frontal lobes fired up! I pretty much talk myself through it: "Ok, so there goes my amygdala kicking in... those yacky feelings are all of the adrenaline and cortisol whooshing around my body... It's just trying to protect me... breathe... keep breathing... ok, now feeling calmer, back to being able to think rationally."

So next time you're getting ready for the presentation or interview of your life, remember this. Oh, and while were at it, in that specific scenario, you know I mentioned at the top of this section that the amygdala draws meaning from emotions and associates them with responses? Yeah well, that feeling that you think is nerves... it's just excitement! Both of those emotions 'feel' the same. It's simply the association and meaning we make from them that conditions us to give it a negative connotation. Go make a new association with that one!

———

The Twat Trap - Resentment, Anger, Bitterness and the Green-Eyed Monster

One of my 'suite' of mini courses that I provide is call "The Fuck It Philosophy" - interested? Head over to the resources link: bit.ly/woman-up-FREE-resources for deets (sorry, that wasn't meant to be a plug.)

Back to it...

Is your life full of 'fuckscapades'? Yeah, mine was too! (A 'fuckscapade' is an exhausting experience of fuck giving.)

The Fuck It Philosophy is all about how to let go and not give so much of a fuck about stuff.

Seriously though, one of the seven stages to that philosophy is "Avoid the Twat Trap"

There's a couple of ways you can end up in the twat trap. Firstly, you can end up there by giving a fuck for far too long, to the point where you become bitter, twisted and riddled with resentment. The second is when you stop giving a fuck, but it goes too far, you overplay it, and you become a bit of a selfish arsehole that doesn't give a fuck about anyone but themselves. We all know one... or two.

For most women, there's not a lot of risk of the latter becoming true. Generally speaking we're far too altruistic for our own good, but it doesn't mean it's not possible. Sometimes the AFBFH (the alpha female bitch from hell) detaches herself so much that she becomes a bit of a lone wolf and her self-preservation mode prevents her from getting too close to anyone or letting anyone in. If that's you and you want to do something about it, get in touch.

For this chapter, I'm going to focus on the majority and that's women who fall into the twat trap because they allow themselves to be treated like doormats through their people pleasing nature. Now you might be thinking 'how can you be a doormat and a twat?' The reason? Because the long-term doormat position results in passive aggressive behaviour and passive aggressive behaviour is the most twatish behaviour of all!

You may recall from earlier in the book when I explored what it meant to Woman Up and be assertive, I shared a list of different behaviours that would be classed as passive aggressive and that most people don't associate with e.g.: sarcasm, being flippant, huffing and puffing, muttering under your breath, being two-faced, nagging. These behaviours are all sure-fire signs of resentment, bitterness, anger and jealousy. I see far too many women experiencing these emotions and it eats them up until there's not that much of them left.

I hope this isn't true for you, but it sadly might be. It's happened to me too. Have you ever had one of those mother-in-laws, the ones that snipe and sneer at every little thing you do? Constantly on your case, judging you, making snidey comments at any given opportunity? That's what the results looks like. A woman who didn't live a happy, fulfilling and successful life. She's lived her life through and for everyone else except herself. She can't help herself but meddle in your business. She seeks her significance and status by quashing yours. She is full of toxic vileness. She is a twat. She is a twat because she is full of resentment, bitterness and possessed by the green-eyed monster.

I want to spend a bit of time exploring each of these in a quest to open your eyes to the potential warning signs so that you may avoid the twat trap completely.

Resentment and Bitterness

Many people don't cotton on to the fact that they're feeling resentment. It's a strong negative emotion born out of feeling wronged by someone or treated unfairly in some way. It's also actually really common. So how do you know if you're feeling resentment? Those who experience resentment may have feelings of annoyance and shame - they might also harbour a desire for revenge.

Where does it come from? Feelings of resentment may result from the lack of expression of emotions after a painful experience. They may come from a true, imagined, or misunderstood injustice. What I mean by that is that sometimes, what we resent, we've actually made up - it's just a story that we're telling ourselves or let's say, a friend made a comment that we just took the wrong way resulting in begrudging feelings.

Unhelpfully, when we experience resentment, we may feel personally victimised and may be too angry or ashamed to discuss what we're feeling, instead allowing the grudge to fester and be expressed in the form of passive aggressive behaviour like sulking and sarcasm.

Given I said that many people don't cotton on to the fact they're at the raw edge of resentment, you may find it useful to know some of the classic signs so you can check in to see if it's showing up for you:

- Continual or recurring feelings of a strong emotion, such as anger, when thinking about a specific interaction or experience.
- Feelings of regret.
- Fear or avoidance of conflict.
- Tense relationships.
- Feeling invisible, inadequate, or less-than.
- Keeping 'score' in a relationship.
- Unbalanced power dynamics in a relationship.
- Caring for someone else and not having your own needs met.
- Hurtful words from someone.

Our job here, as the title of this section suggests, is to avoid that passive aggressive twat trap and that's not always easy. At a basic level it requires you to 'let go'.

In many cases, letting go of resentment means forgiving. It most likely means adjusting your frame of mind or emotional responses.

To let go of resentment, it may help to:

- Consider why letting go is difficult. What feelings come up when you consider moving on from the resentment? Letting go of resentment can trigger fears of losing something about yourself e.g., identity, especially when the resentment has been held in for a long time.

- Use self-compassion. One that I really struggle with myself and had a whole therapy journey around. We find it pretty tough to be kind to ourselves, yet we'd easily be able to do it for others. My lesson here was to learn to talk to my 'child' self as that allowed me to be much kinder than I would to my adult self. It's also worth a watchout around when we hold on to resentment for long periods of time - we find that the emotions associated with the resentment, such as anger or regret, also provide a sense of security or familiarity and this makes them doubly tricky to alleviate.
- Change your frame of reference. When the resentment 'stich' was caused by a misunderstanding, or the person who did something hurtful does not understand what they've done, trying to see things from their perspective may help reduce resentment.
- Practice gratitude. When feelings of resentment start to bubble up, try listing things you're grateful for. This gives you some space to step out of 'victim' mode so that you are ready to take some positive action.

WARNING - If neglected, resentment can become toxic if you bury it within you for long periods of time! ACT FAST!

Jealousy/Envy

For me, there is nothing uglier than female jealousy and the way it manifests itself is poisonous. We've all experienced a good old attack of the green-eyed monster at some point in our lives, I think that's natural, but the way in which we handle it, and ourselves, can make or break the situation, sometimes even crushing relationships between friends completely.

Jealousy is a flippin really complex emotion and can play out in many ways like suspicion (v common indeed), rage, fear, even humiliation. These feel yacky and therefore our natural tendency is to bury them and try to pretend that they're not happening #schoolgirlerror.

Whilst the classic scenario that springs to mind for many is the romantic relationship between two lovers, jealousy is experienced in all kinds of relationships, think of siblings and colleagues at work too. What causes it? It often stems from feeling abandoned or due to low self-esteem or high neuroticism.

I've experienced it myself quite a lot lately. Here am I working hard to get the business I'm hugely passionate about off the ground (any help gratefully received btw – just recommend this book to someone you know... job done!) and yet I feel encompassed by others speeding past me with no effort at all, feet up on the dash, filing their nails – FFS! And I don't like it!!! Even more, I don't like me for how I react. So, what the feck is going on there? Let's explore...

Upon investigation, it's a perfectly normal human reaction is envy (ooh, that was very northern, weren't it?). Envy and jealousy are emotions. They are different though, but can be addressed in the same way. Envy is a reaction to lacking something whilst jealousy is a reaction to the threat of losing something – opposite sides of a coin, I guess? Envy is known as "The art of counting someone else's blessings instead of your own."

These emotions are NOT BAD. They do not make you a bad person. They are extremely uncomfortable emotions which cause our self-worth to plummet. I've talked many times before about the fact that as human beings, we are ultimately driven in everything we do by a quest for self-worth. Every action, every behaviour is chasing that goal. That doesn't mean we always get it right though. Sometimes wonky application occurs! That's often due to the stress of feeling shame, guilt, embarrassment even, for feeling envious. Our defence mechanism kicks in and we go into self-preservation mode. That's when we start acting like a twat. Envy and jealousy are one of the most potent causes of unhappiness. No wonder it gets labelled "The Green-eyed Monster". But that's not true – not if you choose to look at it through a different lens anyway.

We're warned of the danger of comparison, getting sucked into the black hole of 'never enough'. Primarily the blame these days is laid at door of Facebook and Instagram and possibly other more 'down with the kids' social media platforms that I have no clue whatsoever about, but my kids do! Through that different lens though, we can use it to our advantage. Generally speaking, when we feel envy or jealousy, we're not wishing horribleness on the other person, we're still a good human and want that person to be happy. We just unknowingly ache for what they have got! And if we could just see it, there would be the pivotal moment that would be the catalyst to make the shift from envy to inspo!!!

Envy's real job is to help us learn lessons and grow. We can use it as evidence to know that what you want is actually possible! To move it on from being a sub-conscious pipe dream into full throttling, hard-core action towards a goal!

So, if you are experiencing envy/jealousy over someone else's relationship, financial situation, career, business, child spawning... whatever, then here are my top tips to turn that envy into inspo:

1. Have some fucking compassion for yourself, will you! Cut yourself some slack. There is nothing to be gained from beating yourself up about it. Move the fuck on and be kind to yourself. It is a NORMAL, HUMAN EMOTION.

2. Step off the 'Gram' – take a digital detox from all that false reality bollocks. Go and look at some real shit for a while – like the sky and the clouds, some animals, some nature – the big, wide world is awaiting!

3. Question the emotion – check in with what's exactly going on for you – what's it firing up in your belly? Is it envy? Is it jealousy? Is it something else? Whatever it is, put a fucking sticker on it so you know, and it knows, what it is.

4. Dig deep – here comes the tough and tricky bit. What is it telling you about yourself? What is it that it says about your dreams that you may have been neglecting? What have you been burying? Denying? Hiding from? Scared of? Uncover those passions and dreams.

5. Reframe your thinking – let me remind you of the point of envy. It is not to make you feel shitty. It is to help you learn and grow. So let it! Correct any wonky beliefs that may exist by having a stern word with yourself in the mirror!

6. Set goals and go after them! Start small – what's the

one thing you can do every day to move yourself forward towards achieving that goal.

7. Practice gratitude – be thankful for the things in your own life. A starter for ten? YOU ARE ALIVE!!! Live the fucking thing! Remember... envy is the art of counting someone else's blessings instead of your own. Just start counting your own.

Life is so much better when you're not being a twat! Oh... and if you're thinking "well what about if someone else is being a twat towards me?" Remember... behaviour breeds behaviour. Role model this to them for starters, then hold the space and make it easy for them to do it too.

———

Fucking Hormones!!!!!

Hormones have got a lot to answer for, haven't they? They turn us into crazy creatures in our teenage years, blubbering wrecks after childbirth and then a flipping psycho when it comes to perimenopause!

Having experienced all three, I now feel suitably qualified to have a decent opinion on this topic, plus I have a fabulous friend who is a women's health specialist - big shoutout to Marianne Killick! She's our Hormonal Balance expert in Ladies Life Lounge. (You can find her at @marianne_killick_-coaching. If this topic really speaks to you, I highly recommend you go and check her out.)

Let's pop back to that classic scenario that clients bring to me...

66 *"I've been told I'm too emotional in the workplace."*

They're typically in their 40s, in a mid to senior leadership position and floundering significantly. They're on the absolute fucking edge holding on for dear life! (Or their family thinks they've actually turned into a dragon.)

I've helped lots of menopausal women deal with situations like this with great success. They're almost scared of their own emotions and reactions and don't trust themselves to be able to stay in control.

They talk about symptoms such as mood swings, depression, worsening premenstrual tension (PMT), anxiety, panic attacks, anger, snappiness, short temper, irritation, crying and impatience and it takes over their lives. They describe themselves 'like a bear with a sore head', 'getting very ratty', or 'flying off the handle' at the slightest thing. And I can be this woman too for ten days of my menstrual cycle - days 19 - 26 to be precise.

These emotions really threaten our sense of balance and well-being. They use phrases like 'this isn't me', 'I'm not the way I'd normally be', 'it's not like me', 'normally I'm quite a sensible person' to describe this new, changed identity. Have you ever found yourself 'crying over things' which wouldn't have bothered you before? Confused by irrational emotions, women understandably wonder 'what's happening to me?'

Here's something that might make you chuckle; it may even resonate (please tell me I'm not alone on this one!). Like clockwork, 10 days before my period is due, my husband says I get this 'look' on my face - he calls it my "spikey" face. Apparently, it looks like a death stare and I'm about to explode and rip someone's head off. I'm snappy and irritable and I have absolutely zero self-awareness about this. It bites me on the bum every single month! Anyone else like me? Particularly at home, I massively struggle to keep a lid on emotions and its exhausting! I often put this down to the fact that the love from my family is unconditional, meaning that I get away with a lot more than I could outside of it (there's consequences out there!) Then I end up doing the 'repair work' to restore harmony after an emotional outburst by expressing regret and saying sorry... a lot! I often feel a failure because I let it happen time after time and never learn, then I'm back in my self-compassion (or lack of) cycle.

When it comes to the workplace, anxiety, low self-esteem, loss of confidence and insecurity threaten to undermine women's status. Maintaining composure in the workplace is difficult. One woman I worked with said her 'blood boils' and she has to 'bite her tongue' when somebody at work says the wrong thing; there's a lot of 'bottling things up' going on. We can be left feeling at times that we're 'going mad'!

So, what to do about it? For me it's all about education and taking positive action. Learn what is physically happening in your body hormonally as this explains a lot. And when we understand, we are better able to cope. It removes that feeling of helplessness. Oestrogen is the biggest culprit - little fucker! Declining and erratic levels of this hormones are what generally throw us off course. Lots of women find they can cope with their moods better once they realise that emotional symptoms could be 'part and parcel of the body clock' and 'quite normal' at this stage in life.

Get support - we really don't need to suffer in silence. See your GP and if you feel a bit of fobbing off happening, like it did for me, be persistent (see next section for help with this). In the last three years, I've put in more GP complaints than I've had hot dinners! Ha! Lots of women get labelled as depressed and put on anti-depressants because many GPs aren't experts in this field (or have a shitty attitude and think it's a crock of shit). Now, that's not to say that in all cases there isn't some depression present or that in fact, anti-depressants wouldn't help, but it most certainly isn't the first port of call for me.

De-taboo-ise (new word alert!) the menopause - we are making progress on this one but only really in the media and on TV. We're still not talking about it enough day to day and in the workplace. We've got to normalise this and make a stand to no longer have to 'put up and shut up'. We are not baron beings that are ready to be put on the shelf! In fact, screw that! I wholeheartedly believe that I'm peaking on the prime of my life, where I'm birthing the absolute BEST VERSION OF MYSELF!

Then there's the basics - I'm a bugger for this one too so I'm not going to be a hypocrite, but we're absolute bloody pants at taking basic care of ourselves. I'm talking drinking some flippin water, cutting down on sugar, eating nutritionally balanced food, getting some exercise, resting and sleeping well, cutting down on alcohol. God! Believe me, a part of me is furious that this has boiled down to the reduction of my two greatest pleasures in life - prosecco and cake - but it's time to reframe the pleasure I actually take from them. It's not all it's cracked up to be (plus at the grand old age of 42, perhaps it's time I finally grasped the concept of 'everything in moderation').

I've shared this with you earlier in the book but it's worth a point out in this different context...

Here's a really simple technique to help with handling yourself when your hormones are raging and as a result your emotions are getting the better of you. It starts with being able to recognise and label the emotion that you're experiencing and where you feel it in the body. For example, worry in your tummy, anger in your chest, excitement/nervous in your veins, frustration in your head. Once you can spot an emotion and know what it is, the trick is to describe it rather than demonstrate it. This prevents you from having an outburst but doesn't mean you have to leave your emotions at the door. You could be in a meeting and feel very frustrated at the lack of progress. That might make you feel like crying but if you do, people misread that signal. Instead, you're able to articulate it: "This project is significantly behind schedule and is at risk of going massively over budget. I'm extremely frustrated and cross right now about the lack of accountability in this team". That clearly states where you're at without going bat shit crazy or being labelled an emotional wreck. If you're experiencing brain fog as a menopausal symptom and you're being challenged with lots of questions by stakeholders, take control and own it by saying "I'd like some time to reflect and consider my thoughts to be sure I give you the right recommendation to land this change successfully, so I'll come back to you by lunchtime".

Final message on hormones... take some action! You do not have to put up with this.

———

Resilience, Tenacity and Grit

This is one of my fave topics. Why? Because it's a lost art. The world would be a much better place if we all turn the dial up +1 on our ability to stick with things and not throw the towel in at the first signs of a bit of hard graft.

Societally, we've landed at a place where all we want is EASE - our desires to appear at the click of the fingers, at the speed of lightening, with little to no effort – oh, hello Amazon! THIS IS NOT GOOD!!! Yes, I know you love it and it's convenient, but nobody can stick with something that's a bit tricky these days. Imagine what it will be like by the time our 'entitled' children are our age?? Doesn't even bear thinking about!

So, I'm all about driving the resilience, tenacity and grit agenda. Let's discuss...

It's probably a good idea to do the clarity piece of what we mean by these words. We'll start with resilience as, in my experience, people often get muddled up with what this truly is. Here's a little table which I think will explain nicely in terms of both what it is and is not:

What it's NOT	What it IS
Surviving	Thriving
Stoically powering on	Agile, flexible and adaptable
Coping and managing to keep your head above water	Optimistic and seeking opportunity
Flopping on the sofa feeling like you've been dragged through a hedge backwards, necking a bottle of wine and congratulating yourself that you are still alive!	Perseverance, tenacity & grit
	Protect physical & mental wellbeing
	Build on strengths, mitigate gaps and asks for help when needed

So, as you can see, at a basic level, resilience is about being able to thrive though periods of change and adversity, not just survive and living the "dragged through a hedge backwards" lifestyle which many of us are (me included on a regular 3 monthly cycle).

I also want to take you back to the definition of assertiveness. If you recall, one of the bullets of the definition was "To be confident and positive in a persistent way". In my book, persistence beats resistance, just ask any three-year-old.

Lots of women I come into contact with are actively looking to develop their resilience - big tick! That's fabulous in itself. Thing is, they're struggling and finding it hard - why? Because they're trying to develop it WHILST they're going through a taxing situation or period in their life and there lies the issue. It's super tough to build resilience when you're already in the midst of a storm. The best time to develop your resilience is when the seas are calm so that your vessel (that's you) is "ship shape" (excuse the pun) when it encounters a storm at sea. That means doing the graft while life is peachy, but the law of the sod says, who thinks about developing resilience when life is a bed of roses???

If you're a woman wanting to brush up in the resilience stakes, I recommend you start in a period of calm and tranquillity (if you ever have one that is!). When you do, here are the things you are best to focus on:

1. Being able to turn pressure into performance. You've learnt lots already if you've read this far about managing your stress hormones of cortisol and adrenaline. That's a good first step. Then, it's about being able to untwist any twisted thinking patterns you may be at the mercy of. For example:

- Inappropriate beliefs.
- Too high expectations of others.
- Catastrophising.
- Over-generalising.
- Discounting the positive.
- Mind reading.
- Predicting the future/scaremongering.
- Black and white thinking.
- Taking things personally.

These are all 'twisted thinking' examples. If some of these feel familiar to you then your job is to challenge your thinking patterns in order to untwist them. Ask yourself the question "What would be a more effective response in order for me to turn this pressure into performance?"

When under pressure, coal produces a diamond!

2. Self-belief - "If you think you can or you think you can't, you're right!" - Henry Ford.

Self-belief is faith and trust in yourself that you are competent and capable to do something. The signs that you have strong self-belief are doing things that you believe are right, being willing to admit when you're wrong and being willing to walk away from bad situations or relationships.

Some Top Tips to help you build your self-belief:

Focus on what you're flippin brilliant at!

Fail fast!

Girl, get some grit! (More on this shortly.)

3. Motivation - As human beings, we are deeply driven by a sense of self-worth, that what we do every day makes a difference. This is about knowing our true drivers for motivation (tip - it's not money!) and being able to meet those needs healthily. If you feel like this is something you could do with some work on then head to the chapter on relationships, specifically the one with yourself! And also pop back to where I shared human needs in Power, as I mentioned it there briefly too.

4. Humility - This means to be humble, modest and have gratitude, have the ability to recognise when you need help and support, protecting your own physical and mental wellbeing. Generally speaking, we're all pretty pants at this. Why don't we seek help? - Pride and shame (the next section of this chapter.)

To develop humility:

•Self-awareness - spot the signs of when you need help before the shit hits the fan.

•Recognise the feeling of shame and sit in it rather than fight it - it will pass.

•Surround yourself with people who care, who you trust and who are skilled to help you.

5. Focus - The power of focus says this:

If you want to achieve excellence in anything you do, the following rules apply in terms of how many things you can be focused on at once.

- 1-3 things = Excellence
- 3-10 = Mediocrity
- 10+ = Bloody good luck to you!

I've yet to meet anyone who says they want to achieve mediocrity in life! Oh, you too? Thought so. I know, it's hard though, isn't it? With so many things vying for your attention. Well multi-tasking is a myth in my book. t's a total false economy. Here's a few simple things that you can do to be more focused and ultimately deliver with speed and excellence (this means you can still achieve ALL the stuff, in the same period of overall time AND to a higher quality and standard. BOOM!):

1. Work on one thing at a time.
2. Time block.
3. Take breaks and drink water.
4. Be present and practise mindfulness.
5. Exercise and eat healthy fats - avocados are your BFF!

So that's resilience. What about tenacity and grit?

I know I said earlier than persistence beats resistance, and that it still true. However, tenacity trumps persistence every day of the week. Why? You've heard the saying:

 "The definition of insanity is doing the same thing repeatedly and expecting a different result."

Right? Think that's an Einstein quote if I'm not mistaken. Or the other classic...

"If you always do what you've always done then you'll always get what you've always got."

Well, persistence sits in this camp in that, yes, it doesn't give up in the hope that eventually it will work. Tenacity, on the other hand, is a bit different. It lends itself more to the term "work smarter, not harder". People with tenacity are strategic thinkers and are constantly re-evaluating their approach, tweaking their methodology using feedback, data and insights (ooh, sounds all scientific now, doesn't it?) but there is a big difference in success rates between those that persevere and those that are tenacious.

Then there's grit. Oooh, I find this one of the most appealing words in the English language! Like "moist", it's one of the words that sounds like what it actually means. Uh! I feel a big word coming on, not my usual style... I think they call it onomatopoeia, where a word sounds like what it means??? Sorry, off on a tangent!

3,2,1... back in the room. Grit means courage, resolve or strength of character. In her book, "Grit", Angela Duckworth is on a mission to answer a single question "Who is successful and why?" In a very small nutshell, here's what she discovers...

Grit is about EFFORT. Effort is worth more than talent. In fact, where talent counts once, effort counts twice.

A simple equation brings this to life:

Talent x Effort = Skill

Skill x Effort = Achievement

Angela explores four key elements to developing Grit:

1. Develop a fascination about what's important to you or you are passionate about.
2. Daily improvement - compete with who you were yesterday.
3. Have a greater purpose/meaning (Think like the cleaning guy from NASA - he doesn't clean toilets; he helps put men (and women) on the moon.)
4. Have a growth mindset - this means having a belief that you can always learn, however old you are, and being able to scrap the notion that ability is fixed.

I hope after working though all of this, you can see just how important resilience, tenacity and grit are to being able to Woman Up. These women really stand out as admirable, credible and influential and I guess you're reading this book because you'd like that for yourself too?

Go get gritty!

PS. Watch Angela Duckworth's TED talk or read her book!

PPS. There's a resilience questionnaire/self assessment thingy on my resources link if you fancy seeing how well you fare! bit.ly/woman-up-FREE-resources

———

Pride Comes Before a Fall

Funny saying this isn't it? Ultimately, it's not pride I want to talk about here, it's shame.

Typically, the word pride is associated with men. Men are "too proud" to admit when they're wrong etc. We also label them as having a big ego (I'll say a bit more on ego shortly). We don't talk about pride as much from a female perspective but that doesn't mean it isn't there. Pride is an emotion, both a self-conscious emotion as well as a social emotion. It's about stature - our reputation gained by ability or achievement. Pride reflects an increase in stature and shame reflects a decrease. It's important to note that I do not use the terms high or low here but increase and decrease and that's what's important, whether it goes up or down, not the actual level of it.

Why do I have so much to say about this? Because it's been a painful journey for me. I've mentioned my own therapy a few times in different contexts and this is a big part of that. A culmination of my childhood and upbringing, relationship with my dad, the pecking order with my siblings and step siblings, and my career experiences have all led to high performance syndrome based on unrealistic expectations I've placed on myself and that others have placed on me too.

As a small child, I was the eldest. In fact, I was an only child till I was 7. I didn't have a very close relationship with my dad; I was told to be quiet while he sat in his armchair reading the paper or watching sport on TV. He didn't engage with me that much and I craved his attention, especially once the blue-eyed boy, my younger brother, arrived (Jeepers! I even tried to kill him off by giving him a piece of Blackpool rock when he was 6 months old and nearly choked him to death!). Dad (and Grandad) finally had their little football pal. Now I had to work even harder to get noticed. A lot of the time, I just gave up.

In my teens, we became a stepfamily after my parents divorced and I inherited a stepsister, 18 months my junior, and an older stepbrother who had already left home, so he didn't feature too much. This is where things really became evident. I was held to a completely different standard to the rest of them. I was sent to a different (read better) school, wasn't allowed out till I had done my homework, had big expectations of GCSE grades, was taught the value of money very seriously e.g., if I borrowed 50p for the bus, I had to pay it back with interest. Meanwhile, my slightly younger stepsister went to the local comp, had no pressure about exam grades and was financially supported whenever the situation arose or the shit hit the fan! By the time I was 18, I had my own mortgage, a great job, a cool little car - I was completely independent. I remember getting a phone call from my dad one Sunday to tell me that my younger step sister was pregnant and I (yes, me) got a lecture about life not being a dress rehearsal you know!!!! FFS!

I've constantly been on a mission to prove my levels of achievement to my dad, because I want him to be PROUD of me. My husband even says I act differently when I'm with my dad. He says I'm constantly talking about things I've achieved or been able to buy because I want to impress him.

In my career, it's panned out relatively the same. I've been ambitious. As soon as I achieve something I'm on to the next big goal, barely stopping to acknowledge my results. I've always said:

 "I have to be doing a job I can't quite do yet".

I've grown up in large corporate organisations where performance and KPI's are EVERYTHING! Mix that with a number of absolute cockwombles for bosses who just continually demand more and have no care for your wellbeing, I think you'll find it easy to see how I've become a sufferer of high-performance syndrome. The relevance of this? Go back to Hannah Montana - sometimes I'm gonna have to lose and for me with that comes a MASSIVE amount of shame that I have buried soooooo deep and never dealt with.

I've recently become fascinated about shame after having read Brené Brown's book, "Daring Greatly" (one of my fave reads of all time, I implore you to read it too, and watch her TED talk, as I mentioned earlier). She deeply explores our feelings of shame and broadly encourages us to be courageous and lean into that, rather than fight or bury it through our quest to be perfect. Vulnerability is the key theme that runs though this and her quest in the book is to dispel the widely accepted myth that vulnerability is a weakness and instead see it as a strength. Without that vulnerability, we shut ourselves off from revealing our true selves and the things that bring us great meaning and purpose.

So, after immersing myself in this, I feel like I've found my way in being vulnerable, leaning into feelings of shame and being able to hold the space for myself to be proud so it no longer has to come before a fall. What is that all about anyway? I had to google where the saying comes from and what it actually means. According to the Cambridge dictionary it's this: if you are too confident about your abilities, something bad will happen that shows that you are not as good as you think... Which leads me on nicely to conclude this section with ego, as I promised I would at the outset.

Ego is the part of the mind that mediates between the conscious and the unconscious and is responsible for reality testing and a sense of personal identity. However, it often has negative connotations attached to it. Here's why: We all have strengths, yeah? Sometimes, when our ego overplays those strengths, they play out as weaknesses e.g., confidence over-played = arrogance. Given that, as women, we're less likely than men to inflate our strengths (think about the job application scenario - women will only apply for a job if they can do at least 80% of the requirement whereas men are often the reverse - broad sweeping statement I know, but use it as a loose principle), that's why ego ends up being perceived as negative - because often it's men who are overplaying their strengths. It doesn't have to be that way though. Ego is healthy when used in the right way. Once again, I believe, as women, we have the competitive advantage to draw on this - most women I meet would massively benefit from strengthening their sense of identity and are pretty good at reality testing.

The moral of the story - lean into shame, vulnerability and your ego so that that you can stand proud with no risk of a fall to follow.

EIGHT

RELATIONSHIPS

For Somebody Else to Love You, You First Must Love Yourself

I BET you're already sick of hearing this phrase aren't you, "You need to learn to love yourself before anyone else can love you." I'm sorry. Stick with me though, because I'm reasonably confident I can show you a way forward with this.

YES. It does still stand. I'm not going to quash this. I firmly believe that before we can enter into a healthy relationship with someone else, we must first development a good relationship with ourselves. See, that sounds a bit more palatable already, doesn't it? Let's ditch the 'self love' bomb and instead focus on having a healthy relationship. After all, that's what this chapter is all about - relationships. And what better place to start than with a good old look in the mirror.

I'm not going to labour the point too much as I know you likely understand this; you know it to be true and why it's important. Where we trip over though is in the usual place, as it is with most things... it's in the HOW.

This is not about self-care, spa days, bubble baths, etc. This is fundamentally about self-respect. The relationship you have with yourself is crucial to your own wellbeing and also to creating healthy and happy relationships with others. Being kind to yourself regularly is one of the best things you can do for yourself.

 "Caring for myself is not self-indulgence, it is self-preservation."

AUDRE LORDE.

A healthy level of self-respect enables you to have the confidence to set firm boundaries. It means knowing what you stand for and what your values are, and being accepting of both your strengths and weaknesses. Self-respect is an inner quality that each individual must take time to develop. There are some really simple and effective ways to begin to develop your self-respect, but know that some of this might be hard work to do. You're going to be peeling back the layers of yourself that you might not have looked at for a long, long time... if ever!

Figure out what makes you respect yourself. First, look within and question what practices make you feel your absolute best and then make sure to prioritise them daily. For example, exercising regularly, starting every day with a green juice, and being under the covers by 10 p.m.

Be honest about who you are and who you aren't. Lead with honesty. Don't disrespect your talents and interests, YOLO remember! If the 9-5 office job ain't for you... Ditch it!

Stop trying so hard to be "normal". The only way to stand out is to be your real, weird, quirky self. I actually LOVE to know that I'm anything but normal. Being called a weirdo is a huge compliment to me.

Don't let other people define your boundaries. Many people have good intentions, but their advice is often clouded by their emotional baggage. So, when someone tells you "You'll never be able to do that" or "You shouldn't" or "You can't", ignore them until you have figured out for yourself what's true.

Learn to say no. One that absolutely sits in my zone of genius! I love liberating women to be able to say no. (Head back to chapter 5, on Power, for my guilt free formula.) Letting others know what isn't OK doesn't make you a bad person; it makes you a strong and respectable person.

Get comfortable with your own company. This one was a complete killer for me. I detest my own company. I still don't particularly enjoy it but I have learned to be ok with being on my own.

Self-respect is all about treating yourself the way you'd want others to treat you. If we constantly focus on our flaws, we're basically giving the rest of the world permission to do the same and that's no way to start ANY kind of relationship with anyone - work, friendship or romantically.

Do the work on you first.

Human Needs

We've all got needs! Yeah, those type of needs included too (I know you thought about them).

When it comes to relationships, they tend to go pear shaped because we struggle to see the world through each other's lenses - their "map of the world" in NLP (Neuro Linguistic Programming) terms. There are lots of factors that create our own frame of reference, too many to list here but things like our values, communication preferences, experiences in life, all shape our paradigm.

You've probably come across Maslow's hierarchy of needs at some point - a pyramid that starts with the basic needs for food, water and shelter, up to a level of self-actualisation. Most people find it reasonably straight forward to master the basics, but the higher you climb up the pyramid, the trickier it gets to meet your needs because it's not obvious as to how you fulfil that for yourself - sorry Maslow!

I much prefer the work of Tony Robbins (I referenced this earlier) to explore our needs as humans and how they can vary from person to person which enables us to draw a connection between why some relationships are easier than others. He describes six core human needs that we all require to a greater or lesser degree. The trick is in knowing which of the six are a higher requirement for you and what may be different for another person you are having a relationship with, so this can help with your relationship with yourself as well as with others.

According to Tony, "Everyone ranks these basic human needs differently, and the way they are ranked are why you are the way you are as a person. The first four needs in the list below shape our personality, while the last two (growth and contribution) shape our spiritual needs. The means by which people choose to meet these six human needs are unlimited; we seek fulfilment through our relationships, careers, personal interests and more. Here's more on the basic human needs and what they mean."

* The following excerpt is taken from https://www.tonyrobbins.com/mind-meaning/do-you-need-to-feel-significant/

CERTAINTY.

If certainty is one of your top basic human needs, you need to feel secure and safe about the future. When you receive positive recognition, it may be accompanied by a need for certainty that the recognition is authentic and will continue. In order to live a life filled with certainty, your life has to stay the same – a nearly impossible expectation to fulfil. So, you artificially control your environment by changing your expectations or by avoiding new situations or people. You find ways to positively motivate yourself and you aim to consistently deliver the same or better results to receive more recognition. This process provides you with assurance that your actions will either avoid pain or gain pleasure, which then fulfils the basic human need for certainty.

UNCERTAINTY/VARIETY.

Though it's important to understand the beauty of uncertainty, those who experience this as one of their top basic human needs can take it to an extreme. They may engage in frequent job or relationship changes for the sake of variety, or take unnecessary risks to achieve the adrenaline jolt they crave. However, if uncertainty is one of your top basic human needs, you will be unafraid of taking risks and will not avoid new situations or people.

SIGNIFICANCE.

If significance is among the top two of your six human needs, then part of meeting that need includes receiving recognition. This may translate into a desire to be seen, heard and listened to – in short, you want to be noticed. You measure significance by what you believe makes you unique compared to everyone else around you. Recognition provides you with a sense of validation that makes you feel seen, special and/or needed. Recognition is a major driving force behind human behaviour because it provides us with a measurement system to analyse and track our significance.

Those who don't devise a positive way to feel significant may end up taking drastic measures to make themselves feel good, like turning to alcohol or engaging in frequent arguments. Others surround themselves with people that they view as less skilled or accomplished to provide contrast to their own achievements. Either scenario can result in increased significance – but neither behaviour is particularly healthy.

CONNECTION/LOVE.

If connection/love is your top basic human need, you are constantly seeking out a close relationship with someone or something. You truly understand that love wakes you up to the gift of life. This can lead to some incredibly fulfilling relationships, but it can also cause you to sacrifice self-care in order to take care of others or maintain a partnership.

GROWTH.

Those whose foremost need is growth are always striving to be better and learn more. They are very good at their jobs, but tend to move on quickly as soon as they believe they've reached their full potential. Though their constant striving for betterment ensures they will never be bored, they can err on the side of perfectionism and neglect the rest and relaxation they need to keep stress levels more manageable.

CONTRIBUTION.

The secret to living is giving, and those who experience contribution as one of their top basic human needs know this better than anyone. If you have a need to contribute, you will likely make a big difference in your community. However, you can lose sight of the fact that giving should begin at home and neglect those closest to you as you try to change the world.

All dysfunctional behaviours arise from the inability to consistently meet the six basic human needs mentioned above. But you don't have to resort to these types of behaviours if you understand your own needs and psychology. By better understanding which of the basic human needs is your driving force, you can set goals for yourself and implement positive behaviours to help you achieve those goals. Understanding these needs, and which ones you are trying to meet in any given moment, can help you embrace the power of growth and create new patterns that lead to lasting fulfilment.

Core Needs	Resourceful Behaviours	Unresourceful Behaviours
CERTAINTY	Cleaning, foundation routine rituals, organisation, backing self, certainty of self, allowing yourself who you need to become in order to handle the problem.	Overeating, control of others, watching hours of TV instead of having a life, stuck in a rut, obsessive compulsive behaviour, procrastination.
UNCERTAINTY/VARIETY	New challenges, playfulness, embracing adventure, reframing the meaning of events, different hobbies, creativity.	Overwhelm, drug taking, intoxication, changing TV channels, self-sabotage, creating drama and problems for ourselves so we have something to do.
SIGNIFICANCE	Leader of self and others, volunteer work, speaking up, achieving a goal, mastery in our field.	Putting others down, promiscuity, gossip, sad stories about self, martyr, victim, lying, rebellion.
CONNECTION/LOVE	Sharing, supporting others, connect through nature, faith, self-love, self-worth, your truth, unconditional love, interdependent relationships.	Needy, self-harm, unhealthy relationships, connection through problem e.g. drugs, "If you don't love me I'll hurt myself."
GROWTH	Lifelong learning, pursuit of mastery, learning to teach.	Information gathering without applying, learning junkie.
CONTRIBUTION	Paying it forward, donating to charity, volunteering, helping people, doing things for others.	Being a martyr, giving without learning to take care of yourself, giving to get.

My top drivers are Uncertainty, Significance and Growth, in that order. When I'm conscious of this, I'm easily able to meet my needs with the healthy resourceful behaviours. When I'm unconscious, I tend to fall into some of the unresourceful behaviours. It's easy to see how these can support your relationship with yourself but also to understand some of the nuances you may experience in relationships with others. Where there is conflict or friction in the relationship, you will commonly uncover a mismatch in drivers, which goes a long way to explaining why things get a bit tricky.

Spend some time giving thought to your top drivers and to what degree you are meeting those healthily or unhealthily right now.

As we lead into relationships with other people you may also wish to consider what clues their behaviour is giving off for you to understand what some of their drivers might be and how you can support them to meet their needs healthily too.

———

Who Wears the Trousers in Your Relationship?

I absolutely HATE the saying "Who wears the trousers in your house?". What utter sexist crap! Thing is, most people these days don't even realise what they're saying. It's one of those phrases you grew up with which meant 'who makes all the decisions round here'. Well, that could be anyone quite frankly, and has nothing to do with trousers! Plus, trousers aren't really a gender specific item of clothing these days, are they?

Anyway, off my soapbox. Let's get to the important stuff. One of the biggest problems my clients have is with the relationships that are "closer to home", so to speak. Predominantly, their significant other, partner, husband, call it what you will. It's trickier than the one with friends, acquaintances, work colleagues because there's an emotional pull. It's often an unconditional relationship, and because of that we're more easily triggered (triggered? That's a 'down with the kids' phrase these days I believe!).

Relationships of any kind are bloody hard graft. They're tough. And I, for one, have had a fair few relationship fails in my time. What's good about that is that they've now equipped me, in my forties, to have learnt all the lessons and enjoy a slightly more idyllic existence with my 'husband for life' as I like to call him (much like having your forever home I think), also known as Lord Salt and Saint David (for putting up with a house full of women). We grow up though believing that relationships of this kind are like a bed of roses, skipping through meadows, full of romance, joy and ease. It couldn't be further from the truth - flippin' movies have a lot to answer for! But that's what makes it all the more special and rewarding if you choose to see what the challenges can offer you in return.

It will be absolutely no surprise to you that the answer to achieving equality, harmony and happiness in your relationship lies in communication. In fact, I'm now certain it is the answer to EVERYTHING in life. But we're still pretty crap at it on the whole. I used to laugh actually, in an old corporate job of mine, where we'd frequently comment on the irony of being a communications company and we couldn't actually communicate!

But communication is just one word that doesn't quite do justice to the magnitude of the skill. 'Communication skills' is just an umbrella term for about 27,000 other skills. It drives me bonkers to hear people being told they need to 'brush up on their communication skills'. That's not very specific and it's certainly not very helpful.

This book (and my Woman Up programme) teaches many of the skills to be able to communicate with clarity, succinctly and assertively, so I'm not going to dive into lots of those in this section. What I am going to focus on though are the fundamentals, the foundations upon which communication in a relationship can be the right kind of communication, not just done in the right way.

First off, one of the biggest challenges a lot of women face is that they've grown up without having ever been on their own (this was me), meaning that they don't know how to 'be' on their own, to find happiness in themselves. They're constantly looking for that happiness in someone or something else. The most important step in having a relationship based on equality, harmony and happiness is that you respect and love yourself first. It's really hard to do that when you haven't spent time with yourself (see previous section in this chapter if you're skipping about this book randomly).

A challenge that I've experienced first hand, and continue to, is being really hard on yourself, lacking self compassion. If you're someone who has very high expectations of yourself and you beat yourself up when you fall short of those, then you're going to have a problem with yourself in a relationship with someone else. It might show up as a wolf in sheep's clothing though – you believing that the problem lies with your partner, not you – so make sure you check in with yourself here. My journey to self-compassion has been an interesting one consisting of six months of lockdown therapy where I really got under the skin and dug deep into what was going on for me. I'm delighted to report that my relationship with myself, and everyone else in my household, has dramatically improved since doing this inner work. It wasn't them; it was me. (My kids have even told me that I'm much nicer since lockdown - whilst that's lovely, it also fucking also hurts really hard.)

Thirdly, when it comes to undercover equality (the non-obvious household norms), I observe a lot of women who are riddled with resentment and they have no idea about that. The tell tale signs are those that complain, nag and belittle their partners, constantly moaning and scuttling under their breath. For these women, their problem is not their husband or partner, it's their own inability to speak their own truth, to talk about the ugly stuff, to define, communicate and uphold some personal boundaries. They display quite passive aggressive behaviour, huffing and puffing, saying 'I'm fine' when they're clearly not. They almost blame their partner for not having a crystal ball. They think they 'should know' what's up with them. Yes, you might think I'm being harsh. But I'm saying this because I've been that woman. I settled down with my first husband, who I'd been with since school. He treated me like dog crap on his shoe most of the time and I believed I could change him. I look back now and can't believe how deluded I was!!! I used to blame him for the way he behaved when really it was down to me. I accepted him like this in the first place. I didn't set any personal boundaries and uphold them. Remember I told you about when he was sitting on the sofa opposite me, with our two daughters tucked under his arms on either side and said to them "Look at your miserable, moody, mother". It broke me.

Anyhow, I took accountability for myself and changed all of that and here I am today in a relationship that is equal, harmonious and happy, albeit with life's challenges thrown in. The difference? I know for sure, 100%, that we can get through anything together because we're able to talk about it properly. We respect ourselves, respect each other, we have deep compassion for ourselves and each other, we both have boundaries that we uphold and we're able and capable of talking about the ugly stuff.

So, if any of this has resonated with you, here are my recommendations:

1. Work on yourself first – specifically self-respect, self-compassion and being able to find happiness in

yourself rather than other people or things. Know who you are as an individual.

2. Be accountable for yourself and look in the mirror before you blame your partner for how things are.

3. Remember that trousers are a gender fluid item of clothing. Equality, harmony and happiness come from being able to talk, talk and talk some more.

———

Love Languages

Sometimes in life, it feels like we're speaking an entirely different language to those we are in a relationship with - does this happen to you?

Whether it be the human needs that we've just discussed in this chapter, the behavioural preferences we discussed in chapter 6, or the way we like to love, it can definitely feel like you're speaking Spanish and the other speaking French sometimes. We've explored what's going on with the first two, but now we're getting into the realms of the relationships with those we love, and there is such a thing as love languages would you believe!

This really does begin to explain why we can be in a relationship with someone for decades and still feel like we're just not connected sometimes. It happens to me and my husband ALL. THE. TIME. When we fall out and we have an argument we struggle to resolve, it's sometimes because we feel like we're just not on the same page and almost like we want different things. It doesn't take a rocket scientist to work out that great relationships flourish when we understand each other better. That's easier said than done, especially when you're consumed with red mist in the middle of a barney.

In his #1 New York Times bestseller, "The 5 Love Languages®", Dr. Gary Chapman presents a simple truth: relationships grow better when we understand each other. Everyone gives and receives love differently, but with a little insight into these differences, we can be confidently equipped to communicate love well. This is true for all forms of relationship – for married or dating couples, for children and teenagers, for friends and co-workers, for long-distance relationships, for those brand-new loves and for the romances that are older than the hills.

This stuff BLEW MY MIND! It was so simple I had no clue why I hadn't realised it before! If you've not come across them either, you're gonna LOVE this! (And if you have, maybe you've forgotten about it and this refresher will serve you well.)

1. Words of affirmation.

People with words of affirmation as a love language value verbal acknowledgment of affection, including frequent "I love yous", compliments, words of appreciation, verbal encouragement, and often frequent digital communication like texting and social media engagement.

2. Quality time.

People whose love language is quality time feel the most adored when their partner actively wants to spend time with them and is always down to hang out. They particularly love when active listening, eye contact, and full presence are prioritised hallmarks in the relationship. This means giving undivided attention - no TV, phones etc., just meaningful conversations.

3. Acts of service.

If your love language is acts of service, you value when your partner goes out of their way to make your life easier. It's things like bringing you soup when you're sick, making your coffee for you in the morning, or picking up your dry cleaning for you when you've had a busy day at work. This love language is for people who believe that actions speak louder than words.

4. Gifts.

Gifts is a pretty straightforward love language: You feel loved when people give you "visual symbols of love," as Chapman calls it. It's not about the monetary value but the symbolic thought behind the item. People with this style recognise and value the gift-giving process: the careful reflection, the deliberate choosing of the object to represent the relationship, and the emotional benefits from receiving the present.

5. Physical touch.

People with physical touch as their love language feel loved when they receive physical signs of affection, including kissing, holding hands, cuddling on the couch, and sex. Physical intimacy and touch can be incredibly affirming and serve as a powerful emotional connector for people with this love language.

So, you're probably wondering which one I am and how is my hubby different? My love language is OFF THE SCALE physical touch and my husband's is acts of service. Interestingly, I believe physical touch would be his lowest love language and here's how I know... it's actually quite funny. When I'm craving that physical touch and it's not coming easily, I try to fulfil it by touching him. Given that it's his lowest out of the five, this really pisses him off, especially if I'm trying to stroke him (because this is what I like) as he finds that ticklish and extremely annoying. This seems to just exacerbate the situation sometimes and the barney gets even worse!!!

If this is speaking to you and you're having a mega lightbulb moment like I did, I highly recommend you doing some more research into this and my first port of call would be to take the Love Languages quiz on the website at: https://www.5lovelanguages.com/quizzes/

―――――

Being Assertive in the Bedroom

OK, so we've gotten to THAT section in the relationship chapter. Ha!

The one that we never speak of but we're all dying to know a little more about.

YES... let's talk about sex baby. (Sorry, put the song in your head now, haven't I?)

Whilst we can have a little bit of fun with this, there's also a really serious side to it too. As a mother of three daughters (as I write this, aged 17, 15 and 10), I have huge concern and worry for how their lives will play out sexually. I'm trying my best to liberate them in this department without being an embarrassing mum (and I think I'm failing spectacularly in those stakes!).

My early experiences of sex were a bit, well, Meh. There's no other word I'd use to describe it. I just went along with stuff and 'behaved' in the way I thought I should e.g., what I'd seen in films. It's important to note, nothing bad has ever happened to me (Well, that said, I've experienced plenty of the sexual harassment and assault that many of us have come to except as part and parcel of being a woman that only now I'm realising is completely not OK) e.g. I've not been raped or sexually abused. Why do I feel the need to point that out? Because as I've gotten older, I've begun to learn from so many women around me who have. It is far more common than I thought. In these circumstances, lord knows how you get to a place of even considering being assertive in the bedroom. I do not profess to being an expert in that space. That is one best supported by therapy professionals.

Many of my conversations with friends over the years about sex have carried the vibe of "Uh.... Just hurry up and get it over with". Most say they would get out of it if they could or just "do their duty" to keep him quiet (that's if in a heterosexual relationship) and that makes me really sad. Whilst I also used to be part of this gang, since being in a relationship with my husband, it's opened my eyes to a very different way of being. I really enjoy sex! That's mostly down to my partner being a really thoughtful lover, not selfish in that sense at all. I won't say too much as, if he reads this, he will be mortified at me oversharing (he doesn't even like me shouting to him whilst he's in a queue as people can overhear! I usually only want to know what flavour pasty he wants). Where am I going with this? Well, whilst I'm an assertiveness coach and it's my zone of genius, I still really struggle to be assertive in the bedroom and that's on top of (pun!) having a partner who holds the space and makes it super easy for me to be so. Therefore, if I find it tricky, then I'm as sure as hell that other women are in the same boat.

I'm a firm believer in counting orgasms not calories! (I even have a t-shirt with it on, you can get yourself one in our shop at shop.ladieslifelouge.com), and I'd love nothing more than to convince other women to do the same. I want women to be freed of either putting up with crappy sex or having to pretend to be a porn star coz real sex just isn't like that. Thing is, we can't just blame other people, (aka men) for that. There are a few key things that are important in being set up for success to be assertive in the bedroom:

1. Knowing what you like and what turns you on. If you don't know the answer to this it's time to start exploring. We can't expect someone else to satisfy us sexually if we don't know ourselves. So yes, if you're wondering 'does she mean masturbating?' then yes, you're on the money! (Although if you're new to this, my recommendation would be to start slowly and not go straight for the Rampant Rabbit, as women we're sensual creatures so it's not all about the G spot and the clit!)

2. Then it's time to communicate your wants and desires. This is the bit I find really hard! I get all squirmy and prudish when I have to use 'the words'. The key here is to describe what you want, not what you don't want - remember that from the beginning of the book? It applies to sex too.

3. Guide and show your partner - lots of partners find this a massive turn on, so don't be shy! Give them plenty of signals as to what's working for you. Use positive reinforcement. You don't want to kill the moment by saying "No, not like that!".

And finally, talk about this stuff outside of the bedroom! I've said it before and I'll say it again, it really is all about communication. Sometimes its easier to discuss these things with your clothes on! Plus, it gives you something to get all fired up about for the next time.

I did say there was a serious note to this section, well a second serious note and that's about the next generation of women, our daughters... and actually our sons, now we come to mention it. There's so much unrealistic porn on the internet these days that our children are exposed to, most of which does not help girls or boys to understand what great, loving sex looks like. It's down to us to shape that for them, open up the conversation and be great role models.

———

Toxic Relationships and Gaslighting

Sadly, many of us encounter toxic relationships and not just ones of the romantic variety. Toxic relationships can exist with parents, siblings, friends, family members, neighbours, work colleagues, bosses etc.

We'll define a toxic relationship as: A relationship that adversely impacts on a persons health and wellbeing. Now, that's broadened it for you hasn't it? Maybe before, you didn't identify a relationship as toxic, but with that definition you do?

A lot of toxic relationships are down to gaslighting, a term I've only recently become familiar with but seems to be EVERY-WHERE since Donald Trump's inauguration and it has subsequently been named as one of the most popular words of 2018 by Oxford dictionary. So, what does gaslighting mean?

It refers to the act of undermining another person's reality by denying facts, the environment around them, or their feelings. Targets of gaslighting are manipulated into turning against their cognition, their emotions, and who they fundamentally are as people.

Most of us have experienced some form of toxic relationship, even a gaslighting one, me included, and I'll share some of my tales with you here. The most significant one being my first marriage. You would never think it to look at me today, but I was a right sucker. We got together in Year 11 of school. He was the guy that EVERYONE wanted to go out with. Whilst I was delighted I bagged him, that came with a lot of challenges too in keeping hold of him, and he loved that! He gaslighted me good and proper!!! He convinced me that I was lucky to have him, that it was right for him to treat me mean to keep me keen. He once told me that he would mould me into what I needed to be - and I bloody fell for it hook, line and sinker! I make myself feel sick when I think of how I behaved back then. Very quickly, I came to believe that I was nothing without him. He played away and I tolerated it, stuck my head in the sand, refusing to believe 'rumours' from these girls who he told me were just jealous of me. Yet I didn't walk away. In fact, it made me stick around even more. My friends could shout at me till they were blue in the face, trying to get me to see what was happening, and I just didn't get it. At 23, I bought us a house - I thought if we settled down together, he would change - he didn't. Then I got pregnant and I thought he would change - he didn't. Then we had a second baby and I thought he would change - he didn't. Then we got married and I thought he would change - he didn't. Even the night before our wedding in Mauritius, he left me in our beach bungalow with our two small children while he went into Port Louis, the capital, to go to the casino with his brother. He came crashing in, legless, at stupid o'clock in the morning, waking everyone up. I walked to the ceremony with my dad, followed by a live jazz band playing behind us along the beach, knowing in my heart of hearts that I was making the biggest mistake of my life.

When I arrived and stood by his side, I looked at his hungover face in disgust as he struggled not to faint. I went through with it because all my family had travelled all that way and spent a bomb to be there and I couldn't let them down (I chose to let myself down instead). If we had been in this country, I'm confident I'd have walked out of the church. The marriage lasted 10 months before I woke up one day when I was 27, thinking "What the fuck am I doing?". And I walked out.

My new motto in life -

 "Disappoint as many people as it takes to avoid disappointing yourself."

As I said, gaslighting and toxic relationships can happen with anyone. Here are some common red flags to look out for:

- You feel like you're walking on eggshells.
- You invest time, emotion, money and get nothing in return.
- They hold you back - jealous, competitive, unhappy when you're successful.
- You lack independence - they need to know where you are constantly.
- Your sense of self-worth is declining.

If any of those apply to you right now, here's a starter for ten to help you make some positive progress:

- Learn from my mistakes - stop trying to change them!
- Talk to them about what's bothering you and be clear on your boundaries.
- Step out of denial. Use self coaching questions like: Do I want to spend time with X, or do I feel like I have to? Do I always come away disappointed? Do I even like them?
- Realise that you deserve better (do the work on self-worth and self-respect if required).
- Know that happiness is within YOU, not the relationship.
- Spend time with people who build you up and make you feel good about yourself.
- Accept that this is going to hurt - allow yourself to 'feel' and cry.
- Identify the perks - what is actually serving you?
- If you decide to end it, cut off all communication. If there are kids involved, keep it direct and minimal and

purely focused on parenting together. (I'm living proof that this can work!)

- Heal the shame - do the inner child work - sit yourself on your lap and talk to your younger self with kindness.

Relationships are the trickiest thing we must deal with in life but at the same time, they're also the most rewarding. Choose wisely.

———

BFFs

I want to round off this chapter on relationships by talking about BFFs. I believe having a best friend is one of the most important relationships you can ever have.

I don't have one. That makes me really sad.

I grew up having lots of friends. I was part of the 'popular' crew. But it was all superficial bullshit. As I've grown older, I've realised just how important a best friend really is. They say 'you don't know what you've got till it's gone', and they're right.

Now don't get me wrong. I've got a handful of great friends - you know who you are - people who I feel connected with, who 'get' me, who I enjoy spending time with, who make me laugh. But I'm not able to let them see the deep, dark version of me. There's nobody I feel I could ring at 3am, when I'm in the depths of despair. Do you have someone like that?

I have experienced it though. Growing up, in my teens I had an amazing best friend called Janine. We had THE BEST time EVER! I've so many fabulous memories of the things we did, the places we went... sooo many belly laughs, it's unbelievable! But we grew apart as we entered our twenties. No reason. Just did. We've stayed in touch.

Later in my twenties, shortly after starting a new job, I met Chloe. We were 'forced' together by working in a small team and we didn't get off on the right foot. In fact, it would be fairly accurate to say we really didn't like each other at the beginning. Long story short, we had to hit rock bottom with a bit of a spat and give each other some home truths, in order for us to bounce back and become friends with a high degree of trust and respect for each other. We were inseparable for 10 years. People in work always got our names mixed up: I'd get called Chloe; she'd get called Jodie. Or sometimes, we'd get called Chlodie!!! (That became a bit annoying!)

Anyway, without boring you with all the detail, about three years ago, it all kind of just fizzled out. I've no idea what happened but she backed off. I tried on quite a few occasions to reconnect, meet up, understand what had changed but I just didn't seem to get much back. I still don't know what happened or why. I'm not telling you this to make a big deal about what happened, it's more around the fact that I miss her so much!!! I still, to this day, feel like I have a massive hole in my life! When daft or silly things happen to me, I still just want to text her and tell her. It's a bit like grief. I don't feel like I've got any closure. I probably sound dramatic saying this (I know that's what she would say to me) but I feel like I can't make any more attempts to have contact because it hurts too much when I don't get anything back. If she ever did get in touch and wanted to reconnect, I'd be there in a heartbeat.

So, what am I saying? Having a best friend is a special kind of relationship that's different to all the others, and I think every woman should have one. She (or he) is your sounding board, your conscience, your cheerleader, your shoulder to cry on, your biggest fan, your rescuer, your mirror.

I'd love to hear about you and your BFF. Post a pic of you together on your socials and give me a tag and tell me what your relationship means to you.

PS. If anyone wants to be my new BFF, auditions are starting soon! Ha!

NINE
CREDIBILITY

Smashing Glass Ceilings and Navigating the 'Boy's Club' Mentality

I LOVE this saying that came up recently in one of my entrepreneur circles...

 "If you can't get a seat at the table, build your own fucking table!"

You might be thinking, 'what's that all about?'. I'll explain. One of the many challenges I see women facing in business, professionally and in their personal lives, is that they don't get taken seriously. They lack credibility. And it's a damn shame because in the main, these women are true experts, they have a zone of genius that would add a lot of value and bring something to the party that's actually missing.

There are many reasons for this and multiple factors that influence it. Firstly, there's some self-limiting beliefs going on for these women, a smidge (or bucket loads in some cases) of Impostor Syndrome. In a lot of cases, it's not Imposter Syndrome at all! That's the easy option. But aside from that, there's more, and it's deeper.

For many, I see them trying to break the 'boy's club' mentality without success (and there are some females in that group occasionally, alpha females of course – they've already succeeded in getting their seat because they behaved like the men... note to self – wrong strategy). The reason? They move to a position of passive aggressive – becoming sarcastic, flippant, dismissive. They see it as 'rising above the banter' but they lack self-awareness in how they are being perceived. Result? Zero credibility. The alternative is that they join the alpha females and go 'all in' on being aggressive, resigning themselves to becoming a less than true and authentic version of themselves that everyone can see through, not to mention alienating others who could be their biggest cheerleaders. Worst of all, they're really unhappy, unfulfilled and very rarely achieve the success they wanted.

So, what's the answer? Well, if you're one of these women, here's the secret sauce that will change things for the better, for good.

1. Use what your mama gave you – the strong, innate, female characteristics that you possess will propel you immensely at this point, so don't shy away from them. Use them to your advantage. The things I'm talking

about here are your emotional intelligence, your intuition, your ability to be wholly present and the behaviours of high trust that come so naturally to you. Don't hide these away as if you're embarrassed or shameful about them. Let them shine!

2. Surround yourself with great people – You don't need to 'know' everything. Knowledge is no longer power, that power now belongs to Google. Our power lies in our character. It's personal power as opposed to positional power. Build a team of amazing people around you. Ones that mitigate your gaps or weaknesses so you can focus on capitalising on your strengths. Ensure that team is diverse - that's where innovation resides. Leaders who build clones of themselves and surround themselves with 'Yes' people eventually become like The Emperors New Clothes! In a team built upon diversity, there is friction and chaos, yes. But go back to science, we're all made of the same stuff, molecules and atoms that collide and chemically react to create something new. The constant jostling and vibrating of these particles give us heat, light, and life.

3. Sharpen your saw – one of the wonderful Mr Covey's habits! Keep learning and developing. (Caveat – watch out for becoming a serial course goer. That is not the same thing. Ensure you move from 'motion' to 'action' (Atomic Habits: James Clear). That means working more on the implementation and application of new skills than the absorption of overloading content that just sits in a filing cabinet in your brain gathering dust). What puts you ahead of the game? Bridging the

Knowing-Doing gap. Many people have been on all the courses and learnt all the stuff. They know it. All of it. They can regurgitate it reasonably well if you ask them. But do they do it? Practice it day in, day out? Do they shite. The skills I highly recommend are influencing and, of course, assertiveness (both of which I can help you out with).

4. Be frank with your feedback – No matter how senior in an organisation I explore, very few people are really good at giving high quality feedback. Firstly, they give it with wonky intent. Feedback should be given with super, squeaky clean intent – giving it for the benefit of the other person in a quest to help them get better and/or endorse their strengths to motivate them to do more of it, NOT to get something off your chest because they've pissed you off or given your ego a bit of a dent. Ensure you feedback at behavioural level, not at identity – it should not be a character assassination. You should ensure that you articulate that behaviour very specifically, along with the impact it had. Then remember, this is a two-way conversation. Now would be a good time to listen, you might learn something and then both of you can make any conscious choices you wish (or not as the case may be) to do more of or do differently to get the result or outcome you desire.

5. Snowflake to Sassy – Sadly, many of the women I meet in these circumstances have a stab at challenging their position and boosting their credibility but when it doesn't work, they throw the towel in (snowflake syndrome). Being assertive and to 'Woman Up'

involves throwing some sass around, being tenacious and having some grit. Dig deep. Go again. Tweak your approach. I'll go back to the quote at the beginning of this section... "If you can't get a seat at the table, build your own fucking table".

Knowledge is Not Power - SKILL is!

OK, so relatively short message here but a powerful one all the same.

I mentioned very briefly in the previous section of this chapter that knowledge is not power anymore. Lots of people still believe it is, but they are mistaken. Why? Because we've got Google for that! The t'interweb is full of, I don't know, trillions of pieces of information - if I could be at all arsed, I could google that too, but I can't. Oh, and if Google doesn't know, then you can bet you bottom dollar there's a tutorial on YouTube. (I wonder if in 20 years someone will pick up this book and laugh their socks off at how old-fashioned Google and YouTube sounds?) This therefore renders any attempts to store knowledge in our noggins null and void. So, stop wasting your energy and brain power trying to do so. It drives me flippin crackers that the education system in this country still attempts to teach and test knowledge - no wonder we've got a generation of people who can't sort their money out, hold down a conversation or make beans on toast! What should we be teaching? I'll tell you, shall I? Skills and behaviours, that's what! Uh, I'm getting all wound up and stressy just thinking about it, it's a proper soap box topic for me, especially after a few sherbets, namely gin being the main culprit (I can maintain a grip on it if it's prosecco).

Anyhow, back to the point. So, knowledge is no longer power, skill is. So next time you're going into a meeting or to pitch to a client, quit flapping about whether you know all the answers to every possible question you might get asked because that's not where your credibility lies. Your credibility lies in your level of skill to facilitate, influence and have presence, to name but a few. It's how you 'field' those questions that matters.

The End. (Of that topic, not the book obvs, we've still got a fair bit of ground to cover.)

———

Demonstrating Authority in your Zone of Genius

You'll have heard me use this term "zones of genius" a few times throughout this book already, but what does it mean? I know it can sound a bit 'buzzwordy' but it has got a real and practical connotation for me.

So, what is one? Your zone of genius is what's most effortless for you. It's not just what you're passionate about or what you're kinda decent at. I'll expand on this further in a moment.

First, it will be useful to understand why you would even want one in the first place. Well, for many women, whether in an ambitious corporate career or an entrepreneur growing her empire, there is a requirement for you to stand out and be noticed. Sadly, for a number of women, we end up standing out for all the wrong reasons - either as an emotional basket case or a nice bit of office totty. There's only one way to handle this and it's to get in the driving seat of demonstrating your authority. By authority, I don't mean being in charge. I mean demonstrating that you're shit hot at what you do. We become an 'authority' on our subject matter expertise.

So, the zoney geniusy whatcha-ma-callit - what's that all about then? Let's explore a range of zones...

Gay Hendricks identified four different zones of function in his book, "The Big Leap".

1. The zone of incompetence: In this zone, you are engaging in something you inherently do not understand or are not skilled at.
2. The zone of competence: In this zone, you are doing

what you are efficient at, but recognise that many people are likewise efficient at it, thus not distinguishing your capabilities in any significant way.

3. The zone of excellence: In this zone, you are doing something you are tremendously skilled at. Often, the zone of excellence is cultivated, it's practiced and established over time.

4. The zone of genius: In this zone, you capitalise on your natural abilities which are innate, rather than learned. This is the state in which you get into "flow," find ceaseless inspiration, and seem to not only come up with work that is distinguished and unique, but also do so in a way that excels far and beyond what anyone else is doing.

So which zone are you in? Most women are typically in zone 2 or 3.

In Hendricks' book, he asks you to consider the following questions:

1. "What work do you do that doesn't seem like work?"
2. "In your work, what produces the highest ratio of abundance and satisfaction to the amount of time spent?"
3. "What is your unique ability?"

For me, as I'm sure you can guess, my work really doesn't seem like work these days - it's like a hobby I happen to get paid for. The way that I work means I get to impact lots of people at the same time and that lights me up. Plus, I'm legendary at it! And that's not me blowing smoke up my own arse! That's feedback I get all the time. And anyway, there's nothing wrong in me coming to that conclusion myself anyway, it's good for me to be able to validate myself internally, not just externally.

If you do find yourself hanging about in zone 2 or 3, or, like I was, you're known for the less than favourable reasons in the work you do, consider those questions for yourself and see what you come up with.

———

Presence

Now we're talking! This is one of my all time favourite topics to work with women on.

In a world where we're always "on" (not period kind of on, like, switched on), it can be really hard to be present. You know if you're winning at life with this one by how often you get guilt tripped by your partner or kids about you not hearing what they said because you we're too consumed with your phone. #guiltyascharged

However, I want to broaden the meaning of presence with you in this section so that you can use it as part of your new found skills and behaviour repertoire, instead of filling our head with all that knowledge nonsense.

Presence is more than just physically showing up. It's even more than paying attention. It's creating an atmosphere that feels like there's an invisible bubble around you and the other person so that, in that moment, nothing else in the world matters.

You know when you experience presence. You can sense it but it's really difficult to put your finger on. Some people just seem to have it in abundance and others just don't. The great news is, I can make it really practical for you so that you too can leverage it to enhance your credibility.

So how do you increase your presence?

I learned all about presence during my freelancing corporate days and it was a game changer for me.

Being present is thrilling, inspiring and absorbing all at the same time. It is the energy you feel when you know you're alive. It is in these moments that we do our best work and create powerful human to human connections that feel authentic.

Patsy Rodenburg is a theatre and actor coach who works with some of the most famous actors in the world, not only helping them to develop their presence to be able to inhabit a role with impact, but also, in the case of Tom Cruise, to have less presence, to enable him to go unrecognised when in public, and also Sir Anthony Hopkins for his role in Silence of the Lambs where intensity of presence was required. What's interesting is how her theory translates to the rest of us; presence is the energy that comes from you and connects you to the outside world. It is when you are fully present that you make your deepest impression on others.

We all have impact. Some people's impact is positive; other people's impact is negative. You will know people who have a very calming impact, others who have an energising impact and those who have an energy draining impact!

Patsy brings presence and energy to life through her three circles of presence.

Circle One.

If you are in Circle One, you are introverting your energy, which means your focus is inward – it is where you are when you are on autopilot, not noticing the little details that matter. Circle One energy absorbs other people's energy and draws outward stimulus inwards. You are not very observant or considerate of the other person's perspective. You are more introspective, reflective and to some extent, withdrawn from the world.

In this circle, 'I give power to you'. I become passive and give in to others, we don't get what we want or need. Our thoughts become self-critical and our limiting beliefs impact how we communicate and connect with others. We believe other people's opinions are always more important, so it doesn't matter what we think anyway.

You are in Circle One if you:

- Find yourself withdrawing physically from people, feelings or ideas.
- Find you are holding your breath or your breathing is shallow.
- You feel left out.
- You feel self-conscious.

By drawing inward, you lessen your impact on the world. You may operate in this circle because of years of abuse, frequent criticism or if you're surrounded by lots of Circle Three energy. You may have learnt to disappear or become unnoticed to avoid confrontation.

Circle Three. (This is my natural circle to occupy).

A Circle Three state is one where you are extroverting your energy. It is like someone is spraying their energy around in a scattergun approach. This is the person with their own agenda, so they may well be noticed, but they are on their own path and it's their path or no path. They talk over people and push their own agenda forward in the conversation.

Circle Three is the Circle of Bluff and Force, where energy is outward moving and non-specific. People who operate mainly in this circle are self-centred, but in a different way – they want to be the centre of attention. We have all come across people like this at parties and all the energy they push out has the effect of making us switch off.

People in Circle Three take power from you. Their aggressive behaviour is based on winning. It requires that they do what is in their own best interest without regard for the rights, needs, feelings or desires of others. A Circle Three operator might dominate conversations with their overly loud voice and over-bearing physicality.

You are in Circle Three if you:

- Notice people backing away from you and giving you space.
- Breathe with noise.
- Are often too loud, either in speech or laughter.
- Don't really notice people or what they are saying.
- You take command of a situation, even though you don't have all the facts.

Circle Two.

Circle Two is where your energy is focused; it is the Circle of Connection. It is a two-way street where you react and communicate spontaneously with others to influence and connect, without barriers or trying to impress or impose your will on them. You are in flow or in the zone, living in the moment. You are really listening to other people and hear what they have to say, which positively impacts levels of trust and rapport.

Circle Two energy represents the perfect balance; it is the powerful, reciprocal energy of true connection, which focuses on a specific object or person and moves in both directions, taking in and giving out. We sense it when we encounter it: it belongs to those magnetic people who interact openly with the world, listening authentically and contributing generously. You can touch and influence people, rather than impress or impose your will on them. You influence them and allow them to influence you.

You know you're in Circle Two when:

- You feel centred and alert.
- Your body belongs to you.
- Your breathing is easy.
- You suspend judgement and remain curious.
- You connect with people and hear what they have to say.
- You start to notice little things about people and what they have to say.
- You acknowledge others.

This might sound really complicated but once you get the hang of it, with a bit of mindful practice, it soon becomes easier and it's totally worth the effort. There are six elements of physiology that, when centred and congruent, really help you to demonstrate strong presence and enable you to become like a magnet to others.

1. Body: displaying open, relaxed body language and making eye contact with the other person, having an awareness of their personal space.
2. Breathing: calm and silent, going deep into the body and using your diaphragm. When you breathe in, your tummy should balloon out (not suck in as most people do when they breathe in, this is chest breathing).
3. Voice: free, open and directed outward to the people you are addressing, not mumbling or under powered.
4. Mind: on the other person's agenda, not yours.
5. Heart: genuinely caring about the other person and the situation.
6. Spirit: a belief that what you are doing is the right thing to do, not cynical or apathetic.

Through practice and conscious effort, you can not only positively impact your credibility, but also the lives you touch, including your loved ones. Try it out tonight with your partner or kids, and see the difference it makes immediately.

———

Surround Yourself with the Lovely People

A common thing I see amongst women is they're struggling to achieve the success they desire and don't know why. They've likely gone through all the strategic and practical possibilities of what could be holding them back but they still can't put their finger on it.

These women have one thing in common - they surround themselves with the wrong people.

On the flip side, a common trait of highly successful women is... you guessed it! They surround themselves with the right people.

But what makes some people wrong and some people right?

I've always loved a quote I mentioned earlier, from motivational speaker, Jim Rohn, who says "You are the average of the five people you spend most time with", so make sure you've chosen the five best people.

It's not a rigid list of what makes people wrong or right to surround yourself with, you've got to check that stuff out for yourself and develop your own set of criteria. For me, my criteria looks like this:

- They will lift me up not bring me down.
- At the same time, they will be frank and brutally honest with me when required.
- To do the above, I must be able to trust them implicitly and know wholeheartedly that their intent is clean.
- They are positive and optimistic people.

- They are fun and have a GSOH.
- They are smart and reasonably intelligent.
- They are non judgemental and enjoy my success as much as I do.

I like to call these people "the lovely people" and so my saying is slightly different... "surround yourself with the lovely people". It's a self talk line I'll use frequently if I feel I'm with the wrong kind of people that are bringing me down and quashing my spirit - I really don't need that in my life.

So, my challenge to you is to check out the five people you spend most time with - are you happy with the average that equates to for you? If not, it's time you got an upgrade. It's absolutely fine to fire them and recruit some new ones anytime you like.

———

Smash the Hierarchy!!

As women, we have enough of a challenge trying to smash the patriarchy, never mind having to focus on smashing the hierarchy too, but in my book, it must be done. I do not care for hierarchy and I don't think you should either.

It's important to get this in the right context though. I'm not talking about being disrespectful. ALL relationships should be abundant with respect, whomever you are, whatever position you are in. We're all just people who happen to wear a different badge and do a different job. Yes, it may carry more risk and responsibility, and you are remunerated appropriately for that (and if you're not, then check out the random situations chapter on asking for a pay rise by subscribing to my mailing list: bit.ly/woman-up-FREE-resources), but it doesn't make you any more important or special than anyone else.

It baffles me how people get all nervous and waffleitis-ey around people who are "more senior" than them in an organisation (or any situation for that matter). In my experience, a lot of this is caused by men. Now, before you go jumping all over me for being sexist, hang fire. Let me explain. Remember a few chapters ago when we were talking about human needs? Yeah? Good. Just testing you're paying attention! Well, I tend to find that there is a higher proportion of men that have a high significance driver, meaning it's more likely to matter to them that they feel important than it is for women.

Why do I believe we should smash the hierarchy? Because it makes for a business that performs better. A flatter structure is more conducive to creativity and innovation, to collaboration and to challenge. Things get delivered at greater speed and to a higher quality.

So, what am I saying? What's my big ask to you, as a woman in leadership? It's this... If you struggle with hierarchy and it makes you all flappy and hinders the best version of yourself, shift and reframe your mindset to allow you to let go of it. Let's let you out so you can shine at your best.

And if you're a leader of leaders who currently leans on the hierarchy, please, remove it. Allow people the space to bring their best selves to work. You'll benefit in the long run, in so many ways!

―――

Vulnerability and Authenticity

In a credibility context, these are very important words. Sadly, they're becoming corporate buzz words that are losing their meaning and being misinterpreted.

Vulnerability is not the same as oversharing. We chatted about the work of Brené Brown earlier and she would put it, "Vulnerability without boundaries is not vulnerability". Her bottom line is this: She believes that you have to walk through vulnerability to get to courage, therefore... embrace the suck. She tries to be grateful every day, and says her motto right now is "Courage over comfort." Her TED talk – The Power of Vulnerability – is one of the top five most viewed TED talks in the world, with over 50 million views.

In her book, "Daring Greatly", Brené Brown describes vulnerability as "uncertainty, risk, and emotional exposure. It's that unstable feeling we get when we step out of our comfort zone or do something that forces us to loosen control." (And in a world full of control freaks, I can see this being a bit of a challenge, 'can't you?)

When asked if she thinks society supports people who are viewed as more vulnerable? Can we come off as weak if we show imperfections? Her response was this:

"The difficult thing is that vulnerability is the first thing I look for in you and the last thing I'm willing to show you. In you, it's courage and daring. In me, it's weakness. This is where shame comes into play. Vulnerability is about showing up and being seen. It's tough to do that when we're terrified about what people might see or think. When we're fuelled by the fear of what other people think, or that gremlin that's constantly whispering "You're not good enough" in our ear, it's tough to show up. We end up hustling for our worthiness rather than standing in it. When we've attached our self-worth to what we produce or earn, being real gets dicey. The good news is that I think people are tired of the hustle – they're tired of doing it and tired of watching it. We're hungry for people who have the courage to say, "I need help" or "I own that mistake" or "I'm not willing to define success simply by my title or income any longer"."

I felt a strong sense of freedom and liberation after reading her work. It sat well with me. It allowed me to be the person I'd always wanted to be but felt I had to bury. Take the writing of this book for example. Five years ago, I never would have dreamed about putting my thoughts and opinions out to the world for fear of judgment and trolling. But as a mother of three daughters, I feel so strongly about contributing to the creation of a society that is good for them and will work for them, that I'm willing to be courageous and allow myself to be seen. I have well and truly stepped into the arena! (Read the first chapter of her book and you'll understand what I mean by this).

So, what about authenticity then? What's that all about? I'm gutted to report that I meet very few truly authentic women. We're too busy trying to "fit in" and "be insta perfect".

I stumbled upon this definition that spoke to me nicely: Authenticity is about presence, living in the moment with conviction and confidence and staying true to yourself. An authentic person puts the people around them at ease, like a comforting, old friend who welcomes us in and makes us feel at home.

I can't stand it when people say "Just be true to yourself, that's what authenticity is about". However, it's probably the best advice you will ever receive, if you understand what it means. A proper cliché if ever there was one! But as true as ever. Be true to yourself means that you are an honest, trustworthy person who lives by a set of morals and values. Being true to yourself is fundamental to living a life of integrity. It does require you to do the work on choosing what morals and values you want to stand by and that's the bit that people often skip over.

However, all that said, Brené's version of authenticity is still, in my view, the best:

 "To be authentic, we must cultivate the courage to be imperfect - and vulnerable. We have to believe that we are fundamentally worthy of love and acceptance, just as we are. I've learned that there is no better way to invite more grace, gratitude and joy into our lives than by mindfully practicing authenticity."

I actually think I love Brené Brown! Have I got a pure girl crush going on, or what? She's my hero!

———

Trust

Trust is one of *those* words, isn't it? Easier said than done.

If I asked you to let me cut your hair, would you allow me to do it? Chances are, the answer would be a firm no. You can tell me at the end of this section your reason why.

It was during the design of a leadership development programme in my corporate days, when we had partnered with Franklin - Covey, that I fell in love with the concept of trust. I finally got it. All the pieces fell in to place and I've since made it my mission to share this learning with anybody who will listen. I proudly class myself as an expert and it is most certainly part of my zone of genius.

You may be familiar with "The 7 Habits of Highly Effective People", by Stephen Covey. Great book! Turns out, his son - also Stephen Covey - was an equally smashing thought leadership guru too. He authored "The Speed of Trust" and I remember reading this book from cover to cover in a single day. It was so enlightening!

See, here's the thing. We know when we do or don't trust someone, but often it's hard to put our finger on why. However, once you can, which this book helps you to do, you're able to leverage the power and, believe me, the power is huge!

Covey uses a really simple formula to articulate it.

High Trust = Speed goes up + Cost goes down + Engagement goes up.

I've yet to meet a leader who doesn't want more speed, reduced cost and a more highly engaged workforce. Oh, you too? Thought so.

What did I learn? Here my speedy synopsis:

Trust is made up of just two ingredients - Character & Competence.

Character being your intent and integrity.

Competence being your capability and track record.

Have high levels of both of these, you'll be a highly trust-worthy person and you'll reap the benefits of the equation above.

He even takes it a level deeper than that through a set of 13 behaviours of high trust leaders, even categorising them into character or competence building - what more could you ask for?

The 13 behaviours are:

1. Talk straight.
2. Demonstrate respect.
3. Create transparency.
4. Right wrongs.
5. Show loyalty.
6. Deliver results.
7. Get better.
8. Confront reality.
9. Clarify expectations.
10. Practice accountability.

11. Listen first.
12. Keep commitments.
13. Extend trust.

Now that really is a whistle-stop tour! But what I want you to know is this...

We live in a world where trust is low - the media, politicians, fake news... to name but a few. Therefore, developing high trust is a real competitive advantage. Not to mention all the benefits I listed above in the equation. To be trusted these days is MASSIVE! It really isn't that tricky if you're generally a good person at heart and work hard to be good at what you do.

I've yet to meet a person who would say they are not trustworthy, yet did you know that 58% of people would trust a stranger more than their boss, according to a Harvard Business Review article? What that says is that people have good intent, but it's always the small things, never the big things, that let us down.

So, let's finish by going back to the question we started with... Would you let me cut your hair?

If the answer is no, is it my character or competence that is the source of your distrust? Can you whittle it down to a specific behaviour of the 13?

If you said yes... Well, all I can say is you're an idiot! (Just kiddin)

———

Feedback

When you hear the word feedback, what happens for you?

Does it make you hold your breath? Feel defensive? Make you nervous, as if you're about hear some bad news?

You're not alone. That's what happens for most people. But it shouldn't be the case. It's only true because most people are pretty crap at giving high quality feedback. Most of our experiences of getting some has been awful. Therefore, no wonder we armour up when we hear the word.

It's kinda understandable though. As human beings, we're hard-wired with a negativity bias, designed to keep us safe and away from danger. Thing is, that served us when we lived in caves and were fighting off sabre tooth tigers and woolly mammoths but I'm pretty sure they don't exist anymore? (I might have seen the odd one in Asda on occasion). These days, it's more our psychological safety than our physical safety that is under threat and that requires a different approach. (I highly recommend you explore psychological safety in much more detail, watch Simon Sinek's TED talk on it.) Our predisposition to negativity means it's easier for us to give negative feedback but when on the receiving end, we respond far better to positive critique. Just ask Supernanny!

If you've ever watched Jo Frost, aka Supernanny, you'll know what I mean. She goes to a family home after being called in by the parents who declare that their offspring are a complete nightmare! She does a period of observation and then sits the parents down. What's the first thing she typically tells them? Yep, you got it. She tells them it's not the kids, it's you. Because they spend all their time bollocking the kids, the kids have learned that bad behaviour is the way to get attention round here. In essence, the parents' behaviour is breeding the unsavoury behaviour of the children.

The first thing she implements is what? No, not the naughty step; that's second. It's the reward chart. The parent's job is to catch the kids doing it right and reward them, not catch them doing it wrong. For minor breaches of behaviour, they are to ignore it. For more major breaches, yes, there is the naughty step.

Well, here's the deal people. None of this changes because we grow up. We just get bigger and uglier.

You may have come across the concept of the emotional bank account. Believe me, it's a much better strategy that using the 'shit sandwich' feedback technique from the 80s! Do people still really use that? Oh yes sir-ey! And it's totes cringe-tastic! The emotional bank account is more of a strategy because it works at relationship level, not incident level. It works on the following premise, like a bank account really. The idea is to stay in the black e.g., putting plenty of positive deposits in to the bank account so that, should the need arise for a withdrawal (to talk to someone about something they need to change or do differently), there's enough in the account to simply make a withdrawal. People respond to this much better as it's just 'normal' and doesn't feel like they're being shit sarnied!

Now, most of us find it relatively easy to give good feedback so go on, knock yourself out and indulge yourself! However, it's still important to do positive feedback in a high-quality way. Here are my top tips, regardless:

1. Check in with your intent - if you're giving feedback to get something off your chest because someone has pissed you off, turn round and go and have a word with yourself. Only deliver any kind of feedback when you can do it purely for the benefit of the other person. It should feel like the giving of a gift.

2. Feedback at behavioural level - it should not be about someone's identity, that's a character assassination. A simple example: If someone is late then feedback they have been late, not that they are a lazy twat!

3. Linked to the above, be specific. So, if they've been late 3 times - Monday by 15 minutes, Tuesday by 20 minutes and Wednesday by 10 minutes - then be that specific.

4. State the impact - what's the 'so what' to your feedback. What's the effect that the behaviour has had on you, the work, the team etc.

5. Be curious - remember this is a two-way conversation so keep an open mind and listen to how your feedback lands with the other person and their version of events. Remember, none of us really see the absolute truth of any situation. We're so blurred by hundreds of cognitive biases that are unconsciously occurring for us that our perception is always skewed and flawed. You might learn something in the process.

6. Remember, it's up to them to decide what to do with your feedback. They can chuck it in the bin if they like and ignore it. Your job is simply to highlight the positive and negative

consequences of their potential actions so they can make an informed choice.

So, having read that, what would you score yourself out of 10 on being able to consistently deliver feedback to that level?

It's an art, a craft. Make it part of your zone of genius plans if you so wish, but please do everything you can to deliver high quality feedback, especially if you want to maintain your credibility as a leader.

———

Being Frank and Honest - It's NOT Calling a Spade a Spade!

A final note to end this chapter...

Many people try to excuse their aggressive behaviour by justifying their crapness with the line "well, I just call a spade a spade". Please be under no illusion... this is poor and it is not acceptable. It does not qualify for high quality feedback.

Being frank and honest with someone is completely different to calling a spade a spade. Why? Because it leads with consideration. It is kind. It has good, clean intent. It is assertive. It puts the other person's agenda before yours. (If you need to, check back to chapter 3 to revisit what it means to be assertive).

Please do not be this person. It's not big and it's not hard. And it certainly isn't clever! In fact, it makes you a compete tosser!

Hats off to those of you who have this nailed and in the bag. Please make it your mission to challenge anyone who you witness abusing this technique!

End of.

TEN

LUMINARY

What Good Looks Like - The 21st Century Woman

RIGHT BACK AT the beginning of the book, I shared with you that part of the Woman Up journey is all about action. That whilst it's great to get involved in protests, marches, demonstrations, signing petitions etc., real change and specifically culture change, only happens when individual people decide to DO something different. It's all about taking ACTION.

In the Woman Up Way, the final step is all about becoming a Luminary Lady. So, what's one of those when it's at home? (Another weird saying from growing up!)

Well, a Luminary Lady is a person who inspires or influences others, especially one prominent in a particular sphere. And that's what we need more of in this world.

I wanted to start this final (official) chapter of this book by bringing to life what it means to be a 21st century woman, if you like, what good looks like. Remember the saying, "what got us here, won't get us there" and just like all creatures on this earth, we must adapt and evolve. That means as women, the future of our species will require us to be different, to evolve and adapt to our environment in order that we may thrive, not just survive.

I've given much thought to what the qualities, skills and attributes of the 21st century woman are and here's my 'shopping list' of what I believe will set us up for success. The criteria for becoming a Luminary Lady is as follows:

- Loves and is proud of the person who stares back at her in the mirror.
- Prioritises own physical and mental wellbeing.
- Places as much (if not more) value on the contribution she makes as she does her appearance.
- Holds a belief that her body is the vehicle for enjoying life, not an object to be judged aesthetically.
- Has her own strong values and principles.
- Respects EVERYONE (including herself) - values diversity and inclusion of ALL.
- Has defined personal boundaries that she communicates clearly and upholds.
- Is strong, both mentally and physically.
- Stands up for things that she believes in.
- Champions and supports other women and has a strong support network.
- Says No to things she doesn't want to do WITHOUT justifying herself.

- Has influence in roles and circles she CHOOSES to engage in.
- Is assertive in clearly stating her wants and needs whilst remaining considerate to those of others.
- Leads with emotion and intuition.
- Inspires future generations of girls and boys to continue to address equality.

How do you stack up against those today? I don't ask you that question with the intent of causing you to judge yourself, but more to give you a benchmark to be aspiring to. Imagine if we lived in a world where ALL women could boldly state that these things were true for them. It would be a very different and much more pleasant world - don't you agree?

———

Lead a Revolution, Not a Rebellion

Choose to lead a revolution instead of a rebellion.

Rebellion sounds like a really cool word. I always wanted to be a rebel. But now that I've given this much more thought through writing this book, it's not what I want for myself and it's not what I want for you, or my daughters.

Rebellions focus on complaining and blame. It's all a bit self-righteous, even when you feel passionately right about the wrong stuff you see.

Instead, I implore you to be part of, if not lead, a revolution. A revolution is about inspiring people to come together to create something new. You build on hope and possibility. That feels much more like what this mission should be about.

It shouldn't feel like a fight. It should feel uplifting and liberating.

So, as part of becoming a luminary lady, I want you to think about what contribution you can make to this revolution. Please don't stand on the side-lines and spectate. Roll your sleeves up and get stuck in. There are trillions of ways you can do that. From simple things, such as role modelling the behaviour I shared with you in the previous section of this chapter, or taking the time to sit and be really present with someone and truly listen to them, to the big grand gestures of charity events or speaking on the radio or TV. Just do something.

Anything.

Work on a principle of small change, big difference - what's the one small thing you can do today that would make a big difference to the cause?

I like the concept of being a Director of Marginal Gains - cool job title, hey? It means to look for the really small, incremental improvements that you can make. When you practice this approach, over time your progress or performance in whatever you are applying it to is off the scale! Try it out.

———

Why Women are Their Own Worst Enemies

Inspiring, championing and cheerleading other women...

OK, so, I listed this as one of the criteria for being a Luminary Lady. This one really gets my goat, you know. I find it utterly crackers that women tear other women down.

IT HAS TO STOP.

If we can't support and help each other, what chance have we really got?

Here's my two pennies worth:

When it comes to discussing how women are objectified and portrayed in the media etc., men are often blamed. We snarl and hiss at men for how they treat women. Now, granted, they absolutely play their part and they need to sort their shit out about that. What often gets missed though, or overlooked significantly, is how women treat other women. Whenever a new series of The Apprentice begins, I can't believe just how catty and bitchy the women get with each other in order to win. And let's not even get started on Love Island!

That leads me to think more broadly and in context with my own life and experiences. I shall share a few of them now...

I found my high school years really bitchy – so much back-stabbing, bitchiness and slagging off went on. It made me stressed and panicky at times. I couldn't wait to leave school so it would all be over. Only it wasn't. It didn't go away once we left the playground. In fact, it got worse. My teenage years were even more bitchy and fuck me, the workplace was horrendous!

I've always preferred to work in teams with fewer women and more men. I've even preferred to have a male boss throughout my career. All because you just never knew where you stood with the women. You couldn't quite trust them or what they said. Outright shocking!

Now don't get me wrong, I'm no angel and I've played my part in that too. It's sad that it's taken me 40 odd years to actually do something about it.

One thing I will point out is that it's in the small things, never the big things so much. Ask yourself now if you're bitchy? Did you say no? I did when I first asked myself that question, but I was wrong. I started to notice myself making little comments about people and their appearance, even just on TV, like... oh god, look at the state of her! And that's it! That's where it all happens. It's in those moments, when we're not even conscious of our actions and behaviour, that it all comes leaking and oozing out of us.

I did a little bit of digging (well, I googled it) and came across some interesting reading about why this isn't learnt behaviour in isolation. It's actually an innate female characteristic. Without boring you with the detail, I read that our bitchiness towards each other stems from a desire to secure a mating partner. Now I get that. But I'm not sure God quite had the degree of foresight to factor in social media and photoshopping into the mix back then. Yes, it makes physiological and biological sense, but over time we've gotten it all sooooo wonky in its application. And we're better and more intelligent creatures than that!

So, women of the world, let's put an end to the torturous way we treat each other. We've enough to be fighting for without the need to scrap at each other. We should be supporting each other, championing each other, celebrating each other and creating the sisterhood. If not for ourselves, then for our daughters and the next generation.

So, it's time for action.

If you are as passionate about this subject as I am.... or have daughters yourself... or have been the subject of the bitchiness... Or have been the bitch (now I'm certain everyone falls into at least one of those categories so no wiggling out of it!) ... get off your backside and play your positive part!!!

———

Networking and Collaborating

Luminary Ladies have great networks and see the real value in collaborating. But these words have been overused and misunderstood, putting a lot of women off engaging in this kind of activity.

I talked a little bit about collaboration earlier in chapter 5, on Power as a foundation, but here, I really want you to up the ante because we're talking about being the cream of the crop here, in this chapter all about becoming a Luminary Lady.

In my view, women are THE BEST collaborators. I've seen it with my own eyes and experienced it perfectly. Collaboration isn't the same as teamwork. It exists on the principle "the whole is greater than the sum of the parts". To be able to collaborate well, you need to be able to lean in and have a desire to serve others as much as serve yourself. It's about being open-minded enough to be able to consider the prospect that together we can achieve more. It's not my way, it's not your way; it's a better way. True collaboration should deliver a win-win outcome. And I think women are the BEST at this!

Why? Generally speaking, we're much more altruistic in nature and are driven by helping others, but there's more than that! There's actually fair bit of research and science that backs my theory up.

An American neuroscientist, Paul Zak, of Claremont University, measured the brain activity of people while they worked. Eventually, his experiments proved his hypothesis that there is a neurological signal that indicates when we should trust someone. Why does this matter? Because trust is at the heart of collaboration. And we've already talked about the value of trust, haven't we? (Please tell me you haven't forgotten already... head back to chapter 9 if you need a recap.)

Our brains are full of neurotransmitters and hormones yeah? One of which is Oxytocin. It is often referred to as the Trust Hormone, the Cuddle Hormone or the Moral Molecule. Why? Because neuroscientists can now show that the release of Oxytocin reduces anxiety and triggers behaviours for trust, love, bonding, warmth, and collaboration.

The neuroscience shows that Oxytocin is the brain chemical that produces the 'I believe in you/I want to help you' effect. It makes it feel good by increasing our empathy for others.

The boy/girl thing? On average, women release Oxytocin more than men. Men release more Testosterone than women and it competes with Oxytocin, so Oxytocin can be stifled. Ta-Dah! Do you need any more convincing?

Now, this networking malarkey. Loads of women are put off networking because it seems to have lots of negative connotations, but that's because it's generally been facilitated in a very 'testosteroney' (new word alert) way. I remember when I first left employment and became self employed, I joined a BNI networking group. Fuck me! That was tragic!

I used to have to turn up to a meeting, called a breakfast session, but it started at 6.15am (that's a midnight feast as far as I'm concerned). Each week, I'd have 60 seconds to say my piece and I was held to account on bringing three referrals of business to other members. It was hardcore! Funny though, I never seemed to get any referrals back. It was all the tradesmen just doing work for each other really, total con if you ask me! And it robbed me of about £800 in membership fees. I'm sure you can guess that I didn't last long! I never wanted to go networking again!

Fast forward 12 years and I have a very different idea of networking: It's just making great friends! Connecting and forging lovely relationships. The day I took the pressure off myself about how I was going to introduce myself and what I was going to say, the magic began to happen. I learned that the best networkers are those that spend most of their time listening and being curious of others rather than speaking. I look for opportunities where I can help others, with no expectation of anything in exchange or return. It just feels good. And low and behold, reciprocity magically appears when you're least expecting it and feels like the lovely treat that it is!

I really hope that convinces you to engage in collaboration and networking. When great women come together, they achieve amazing things! I'd love to hear about your experiences - good and bad - so do share with me on my socials.

———

Turning Heads When You Walk in a Room

Oooh, that elusive effect that so many people crave but struggle to make it happen...

Let's just be clear, this is not turning heads when you walk into the room because of what you look like; it's turning heads because they can't wait to hear what you have to say or are queuing up to talk to you. They want to be in your presence.

Many of the women I work with have a desire to be able to command an audience, to have gravitas and it seems too damn tricky to achieve - what's all that about then?

This is one of those things that you have to step into to make it happen rather than waiting to 'be' it once you've achieved it. That sounds like a riddle doesn't it.

See if this makes it any simpler...

Instead of HAVE - DO - BE, you need to BE - DO - HAVE. Remember that?

This means stepping into the person you want to become before you've actually achieved it. Note: It is not the same as 'fake it till you make it', I am not a fan of doing that at all.

Let's start with what gravitas actually means. Gravitas means seriousness and importance of manner, causing feelings of respect and trust in others, according to the dictionary.

I'm not actually sure that's what all of these women actually want. They've just been told at some point in their career that they need more gravitas by some moron who literally has zilch of it.

What I think most women really want is to be able to have a group of people hang off their every word, to command an audience. That often has very little to do with what you have to say, but more in how you say it. It's about presence. And guess what? I've already shown you how to develop that! Bingo!

I'm confident that you have all the resources you need at your fingertips in this book for you to have an audience hanging off your every word. You just need to believe it and step into being that gal. You got this!

———

Inspiring the Next Generation of Girls to Become Women

Now then, this is proper 'soap box' territory for me.

For the 97th time, I know you know, but I'm gonna say it again anyway, I'm a mum to three daughters. Because of this, it is super close to my heart to do as much as I possibly can to inspire the next generation of girls to become 21st century Luminary Ladies too.

Instagram and Snapchat fucking scare the pants off me! They're turning our young women into shallow beings with little self respect and purely concerned with their appearance. You don't need to be a rocket scientist to work out that this goes against everything I'm all about. If you need a reminder, I'm on a mission to get women valued for the contribution they make, not what they look like.

Now, don't get me wrong, I love to look good, I think we all do to a certain extent. But it never comes before my credibility and the person that I am. What makes me appealing is my attitude, intelligence, opinions, sense of humour, vulnerability, the love I have to offer. I'd rather see people's book collections than their shoe collections.

Instead of getting their eyelashes and nails done, let's show them how to change a tyre and put up a shelf. Let's support them to craft ambitions that are bigger than solely becoming a mum* or marrying a footballer. Let's get them out playing sport instead of having them staring at themselves in the mirror, thinking they're fat when they're no more than a size 6. Let's tell them they're smart. Let's tell them they're strong. Let's tell them they're capable of anything they set their mind to.

Let's tell them they are brave. Let's show them that their body belongs to them and they get to decide what happens to it - nobody else.

Let's stop telling them that they're pretty. Let's stop telling them to be nice. Let's stop telling them not to make a fuss. Let's stop telling them to be a good girl. Let's stop dressing them in pink. Let's stop just offering them the dolls to play with. Let's stop making it acceptable for girls to put up with harassment or abuse of any kind.

I told you I get all 'soap boxey', didn't I? I'll restrain myself at this point. I'll harp on about in on lots of videos anyway, so to get the raw, passionate, full commitment version, go and watch one of them!

*PS. I'm sure I don't need to say this but obvs, I am not saying there's anything wrong with purely wanting to be a mum. I just think it's a little early in their teens to already have settled on this.

———

What Should We Teach Our Boys?

Oh.... And that brings me onto the boys.

I never wanted any boys. I always just wanted girls. I don't know why. I mean, I'd have happily kept one if the universe had decided to give me one but I actually believe I wasn't built for carrying male offspring (slight diversion off topic here for a second, but there is a random theory to my belief - I had two miscarriages in between my second and third daughters and it helped me to deal with that by telling myself that perhaps they were boys and my body couldn't 'bake' boys).

I'm concerned for our next generation of men as much as I am for our women. The stories I hear about how boys behave worries the shit out of me. Their anger issues, addiction to computer games, the porn they watch - they have a really unrealistic view of what sex should be, how women should be treated and what women's 'bits' should look like! And how they're gaslighting their girlfriends at such a young age is terrifying.

A recent murder case on the news demonstrated to me that we're a million miles away still from appropriate expectations around gender. When a woman is murdered by a man, the police tell women not to go out at night. WTF? Why should we be locked up and punished because of the actions of men. Just so we're clear I was equally as outraged by the follow up comments for men to be on a curfew - it's bloody ridiculous! What's really needed is to educate our boys as much as our girls on how to behave in society. And the best way to do that is not in a school, it's in their homes. Role models are everything. Whether they are good or bad. It's how we behave that teaches our kids right from wrong. I know mums who are petrified of their sons. That's wrong. How on earth will they ever respect a girl or woman in a relationship if they don't respect their mother.

So, if you're a mum of boys please, please, please set the boundaries with your boys. Teach them how to treat women by what you will and will not accept from them. This has got to stop. You playing your part as a mum of boys will make you a Luminary Lady!

———

How to Hold the Space for Others in their Woman Up Journey

So, by this point, you're likely smashing it in the Woman Up stakes personally! But hang on, that's not you done and dusted.

Being a Luminary Lady is a lifelong commitment. There's no destination or finish line. Now it's time for you to hold the space for others in their Woman Up journey.

Typically, as women, we're great at dishing out advice and, whilst the content of that advice might make perfect sense, it's often easier said than done. When it comes to this sort of development, shit runs deep. Giving fellow women superficial 'do this' or 'do that' advice won't cut the mustard and in the sprit of cheerleading and supporting other members of the female species, this is your chance to make a real difference.

Holding the space for someone is a weird phrase, I'm not sure if you've ever come across it before but I use it in the context of coaching. Coaching someone is very different to giving advice.

Holding the space is about being loving, non-judgmental and empathetic. Now, what I'm about to share might sound a bit woo woo and spiritual for you but stick with me, it's a beautiful practice.

One of the first elements to holding the space for someone is about demonstrating loving-kindness which is a term rooted in Buddhist tradition. It essentially means having compassion and love for another living being. Primarily holding the space for someone involves deep listening, I've heard it termed 'listening with the heart'. It's more than just hearing. It means listening without preparing your next response. Just to understand.

I often get criticised by friends or family for this one... Having unconditional positive regard for someone. It means that no matter what the other person has done, you still treat them with respect and compassion.

The trickiest part of holding the space for someone for me is to simply sit with what is. It means that just being with the person is enough. You don't have to do anything or try to change anything. Just being there is what matters. Be really present (we covered this earlier) and remember to breathe - it helps you stay grounded and connected to yourself and the other person.

I bet you find it hard to imagine me practicing these things. Yep, I find it hard to do it. But that's not a reason not to. I don't always get it perfect, because I'm human, but as long as I can reflect and say I did my best (the best coaching question in the world, that credit goes to my biz bestie, Roxy, for), then I can settle with that.

If you can do this for just one other woman after reading this book - nothing else, just that - you'll be making a massive difference.

———

What a GSOH Can Do For You

I know! It's a cliché in the dating ads!!!! Please excuse me. But I want to end on high.

A little story... Once, in work, I split my pants right around the arse. Embarrassing, or what? I had two choices in that moment. Be absolutely fuming and humiliated or see the funny side. The outcome would be the same regardless. I still had a massive hole in my pants, everyone could see my arse and I'd need to go home to change. So, I chose to see the funny side. Life is too short, right?

The finally piece in the Woman Up jigsaw and in becoming a Luminary Lady is to not take yourself too seriously! I think you'll have noticed that in me by now.

I measure my success in life by how much I laugh, it's one of my personal KPI's. Laughing is one of the best things you can do for your health on many levels. Having a good sense of humour will be the icing on the cake with a cherry on top!

It's not about becoming a comedian. For me this is purely about being comfortable in your own skin and relaxing into yourself. If you've done all the personal work so far in this book then I'm super confident that, like me when I entered my forties, you'll feel like you have arrived!

You just don't give that much of a shit anymore and it's truly liberating. When this happens, you're able to make fun of yourself rather than feeling humiliated when things go wrong. Loosen up, let things slide a little, see the funny side, take the piss out of yourself.

Some women have been so highly strung for so many years that they find it uber difficult to do this. So, act now, before it's too late! Having a laugh has mega benefits... if these don't convince you, I don't know what will:

Physical benefits:

- Boosts immunity.
- Lowers stress hormones.
- Decreases pain.
- Relaxes your muscles.
- Prevents heart disease.

Mental Health benefits:

- Adds joy and zest to life.
- Eases anxiety and tension.
- Relieves stress.
- Improves mood.
- Strengthens resilience.

Social benefits:

- Strengthens relationships.
- Attracts others to us.
- Enhances teamwork.
- Helps defuse conflict.
- Promotes group bonding.

Mic drop!

AFTERWORD

Parting Words

Phew! We made it! How does it feel?

Do you feel like you've been dragged through a hedge backwards? I hope not!

Remember, right back at the beginning I told you that whatever I do must tick at least one of these five things (obvs delighted if all five):

1. Does it educate?
2. Does it empower?
3. Does it entertain?
4. Does it inspire?
5. Does it liberate?

I truly hope you've not only enjoyed this book, but also learnt something in the process. My wish is that it sparks change in you where you've never dared to change before, but now feel compelled to do so.

I'd love you to share with me if it managed to hit any of those five things for you and if so, which ones. As you know, I'm very keen on specificity when it comes to feedback so, please do share what has enabled that for you. What have you loved? What seeds have I planted in your head that you're furious about and can't get rid of? (The lyrics to Hannah Montana don't count btw.) What has pissed you off? What would you like to see from me next?

It's been my absolute pleasure to pour my heart out to you. Please hold the space for me with it.

Jodes x

PS. I like gifts that keep on giving and so I've got some bonus mini chapters on random situations that you may come across on the crazy train called life - practical techniques and strategies, as well as some fabulous guest contributions from some of my expert friends for you that you can get your mitts on by subscribing to my mailing list, and I'll pop a little treat in your inbox each week. You can subscribe by going to bit.ly/woman-up-FREE-resources

Here's a flavour of some of the topics I'll be covering:

1. How to handle the mother-in-law from hell.
2. Dealing with Deirdre Downers and Fun Sponges.
3. Fending off the saboteurs (AKA jealous fuckers).
4. Avoiding arseholes and twats.

5. Dealing with male chauvinistic pigs.
6. The Epic Fail that is underestimating the underwear.
7. What to do when you feel like chickening out or you lose your bottle.
8. Putting bullies back in their box (includes trolls so this what you'll be on the receiving end of if you decide to troll me after reading this book).
9. Dealing with divorce.
10. Parenting teenagers 101.
11. Accepting compliments.
12. Asking for a pay rise.
13. Saying sorry (criteria for when you should and how to do it properly).

If, after reading this book you'd like to work with me, here's how:

- You can take my short course - The Art of Assertiveness
- You can join my membership - The Woman Up Society
- You can take my signature programme - The Woman up Way in self led format
- You can join my LIVE 16-week signature group programme - The Woman Up Way
- You can work with me one-to-one with a single "Assertiveness Accelerator" session
- You can work one-to-one with me on a 3/6/9 session coaching package
- You can work with me on a VIP basis (with all the luxury perks and treats)

- You can attend my VIP 1-day events/weekends
- You can come on one of my fabulous retreats!

The details of all of these can be found on my FREE resource page at: bit.ly/woman-up-FREE-resources

Love ya. Bye x

Printed in Great Britain
by Amazon